RECLAI

Robin Greenwood,  
most of his early y  
was educated at loc  
School at Tadcast ... he went to St Chad's  
College, Durham University, in 1965. In his student  
vacations he had various jobs: as a farm labourer, a  
painter on an engineering site, a brewery worker,  
postman, and clerical assistant at the British Lending  
Library. During the academic year 1969–70 he re-  
searched Vatican 2 Theology of the Church and the  
Unbeliever at Ushaw Roman Catholic seminary, near  
Durham, and he has maintained a continuing interest  
in the influence of Catholic Theology on Anglican  
thinking and practice. He has contributed articles to  
*Theology*, *The Church Times*, *The Clergy Review*, and  
the *Tablet*, and is a member of the Friends of the  
Anglican Centre in Rome.

After ordination in 1970, he served in the parish of  
Adel in northwest Leeds, and from 1973 ministered as  
Minor Canon and Succentor to the congregation of  
Ripon Cathedral. For the years 1978–86 he was Vicar  
of St Wilfrid's, Halton, a Leeds parish with a tradition  
of challenging and experimental ministry. During  
1985–86 he served as a representative of the Ripon  
Diocese on General Synod.

Canon Greenwood is now working in Gloucester as  
the Diocesan Missioner, Director of Lay Training and  
of Post Ordination Training, based at the cathedral as  
Residentiary Canon. A novice of the Third Order of St  
Francis, he is currently involved in part-time research  
into the nature of Christian Vocation. He and his wife,  
Claire, have three children.

ING THE CHURCH

born in Scarborough in 1944, spent
ears in Boston Spa, Yorkshire. He
al school, including the Grammar
er, until he went to St. Chad's

ROBIN GREENWOOD

# RECLAIMING THE CHURCH

With a Foreword by Alan Webster

Collins
FOUNT PAPERBACKS

First published in Great Britain by Fount Paperbacks,
London in 1988

Copyright © Robin Greenwood 1988

Made and printed in Great Britain by
William Collins Sons & Co. Ltd, Glasgow

CONDITIONS OF SALE

This book is sold subject to the condition
that it shall not, by way of trade or otherwise,
be lent, re-sold, hired out or otherwise circulated
without the publisher's prior consent in any form of
binding or cover other than that in which it is
published and without a similar condition
including this condition being imposed
on the subsequent purchaser

To the people of St Wilfrid's, Halton,
past, present and future

# CONTENTS

# ACKNOWLEDGEMENTS

The author is grateful for permission to reprint those parts of this work previously published in *Theology*, May 1982, November 1983, November 1984 and September 1987; in *The Clergy Review*, January 1987; and in *Ministry*, the Journal of the Edward King Institute for Ministerial Development, Summer 1987.

# FOREWORD

This alert and searching survey of the vocation of parishes in England today is based on a fine ministry at St Wilfrid's, Halton, in Leeds. Since World War 2 this parish has pioneered in many directions, and the Church has been indebted to its leaders for publishing their reflections. Certainly the last ten years are of special importance and are here presented with an attractive fusion of common sense and vision.

While the author conveys the need for the routine work required to maintain a community in late twentieth-century English society, he never loses sight of the discoveries of the worldwide Church since Vatican 2, or more recently, since *Faith in the City*, has begun to dominate the Anglican agenda. The role of the minister is being re-defined and re-discovered. To read, mark, learn and inwardly digest this perceptive and often entertaining survey would deepen the thinking of many of the groups which exist to support Christian lay and ordained members of the Church. Professor Adrian Hastings, also writing from Leeds, has judged that "the business of religion in the West seems perilous enough". The reflections, critical and courageous, in *Reclaiming The Church* suggest how the people of God may overcome these perils and pray and live in the Kingdom.

The living tradition of the Church of England is critical, orthodox and full of hope for the future. Our church is concerned to relive the life we see in Jesus Christ in contemporary England. George Herbert's *A Priest of the Temple* and Leslie Hunter's *A Parson's Job* were larger essays on this theme for former generations. Here is a tract for the times, whose readers will sense in its fifteen brief chapters a concern for worship and a commitment to responsibility for the whole community, designed to strengthen personalities where prayer and sensitive friendship are among the fruits of the Spirit.

ALAN WEBSTER
Dean of St Paul's
October 1987

# INTRODUCTION

Shortages of clergy, declining membership, apparent irrelevance to most of society, the alienation of the young, the break-away growth of house churches, problems of money and buildings; these are among the chief headaches of the churches today.

Some congregations feel angry that central authorities have closed their local church buildings, or removed their local minister. At all costs some wish to preserve, as a last point of stability in a rapidly changing world, traditional language, style of church life and forms of service.

Others read the signs of the times differently. Scholarly research has shown a great contrast between the currently accepted church style which is only gradually breaking down, inherited from the Middle Ages and coming to a confident peak at the end of the nineteenth century, and the exciting varieties of the early Church. We cannot just naïvely pick up the earlier ways again, but the present moment challenges us to plan for the future with more of an eye on the first thousand years of Christian history than on the second.

Many Christians have already begun to recognize, in the stripping down of the churches in numbers and confidence, the summons of the Holy Spirit to fresh experiences of mission, sense of community life and corporate responsibility for ministry. However, many clergy and churches operate by responding in a practical way to the random challenges that each day presents, with no over-all plan for the building up of the community as a missionary body. A strategy worked out by clergy and laity together, based on theological principles rather than mere pragmatism, is sadly too often regarded as a luxury for the highly intelligent or the under-employed.

This book attempts, from an autobiographical point of view, to show how groups of committed Christians, laity and clergy together, can begin to build the foundations of a new way of being the Church with a positive expectation of the collaboration of every member, according to their gifts. But this is no great record of "success", whatever we mean by that in the Church. It is the inevitably diffident reflection of one parish priest on what happens if you take the available ecumenical theology of the Church and its ministry and try to put them into action. Nor is this book meant to be a diatribe of criticism directed at the ch rches and the clergy in particular. I share my own hopes and fears not only with my fellow clergy but with all those committed and deeply caring laity who increasingly wish to share responsibility with the clergy. I offer it too, in humility, to those who see no new springtime for the Church in their area, and who are near to despair or have fallen into apathy.

As I complete this book on the Feast of St Francis, I am reminded of one of the stories describing a conversation between him and Brother Leo as they travelled together on a cold winter's night from Perugia to Santa Maria degli Angeli. On such an occasion it seems reasonable to look forward to the simple pleasures of warm food, a welcome, or a dry place to sleep. But Francis insists that "perfect joy" offers no consolation here and now. Perfect joy is not to be found in the holiness of life of the community, nor in great feats of healing, nor in raising those who have been dead four days, nor in immense learning or spiritual wisdom, nor in success at converting those without faith. In reply to Leo's demand to know where then is perfect joy, Francis replies that it lies in arriving travel-stained, cold and hungry at the friary door, expecting to be welcomed, but instead being taken for impostors and turned away without food or lodging. "If you shall bear this patiently and with joy and love, Brother Leo, write that in this there is perfect joy . . . above all the graces and gifts of the Holy Spirit, which Christ grants to his friends is that of self-conquest and of willingly bearing sufferings, injuries and reproaches and discomforts for the love of Christ; because in all our other gifts of God we cannot glory, in as much as they are not ours but from God."

The way of being a parish priest and the commitment of all the baptized that I try to describe in these chapters was not developed without pain and suffering, both corporate and personal. It would have been so much easier for us all to have enjoyed a comfortable and painless church life. On so many sides Christians are receiving new warmth and meaning in their faith, many are being renewed and we are tempted to feel that "real progress has been made" or that the Kingdom of God is just round the next bend. Yet it seems to me that Francis reminds us that still the road lies uphill, and we are summoned by Christ to live dangerously and without the protection of being finally reassured that we are right by God or man.

It is too easy to be simply angry or cynical about the Church. I love the Church of England in which I have been nurtured and in which I have been a priest now for the best part of two decades. There is hope, but not for the churches as we find them on the whole now, and not for them when they try to exist just in their own right. The hope lies primarily in the pursuit of the servant role of the Church. In the power of the Holy Spirit we can be built up again, built up in God's ways and so learn to share as companions in Christ's own exacting but exhilarating task of helping to hold the world together.

I should like to thank all those who have encouraged me both in exploring new paths of Mission and Ministry and in attempting to reflect on them; chiefly Alan Wilkinson and my wife, Claire. I am indebted to Sarah Baird-Smith for her creative criticism in helping me to prepare the typescript for publication. In recording my gratitude to those who have typed several drafts of this book, I would mention Mollie Cameron, Anne McLean, Olive Withycombe and Angela Godwin.

ROBIN GREENWOOD
October 1987

# 1

# A New Awakening

Anyone appointed as parish priest, churchwarden, or parochial church council member, or to any task within the Church today, has taken on a tremendous challenge. We are living through a period of major upheaval in the inherited long-accepted models of the church and its ministry. One of the chief strands in this is the movement of the boundaries between the work of the parish priest and the work of the people as a whole. It seems to be true of all the main churches in this country that they are fairly heavily dependent on paid professional clergy, but also that sociological, financial, psychological and theological pressures are all combining to demand a fundamental shift of emphasis and style in being the Church. It is also true that all the churches, urban and rural, are bound to be affected by the different pressures to varying extents and on various time scales. For one it may be that they have to face for the first time not having an ordained resident minister, for another it may be a great shortage of money, or the perplexing problem of how six villages can even begin to work together across traditional boundaries.

The recent debate provoked by the Church of England report *Faith in the City* has reminded so many churches of their failure to serve the powerless and poor, both in terms of sharing the faith and of ministering to their human needs. Often the comfortable middle-class churches are unable even to see their own irrelevance, detachment and failure to communicate the Gospel message. The churches that seem almost unaffected by the winds of change are either those with a confident eclectic congregation, whether extreme evangelical, catholic or charismatic, highly motivated to pay their way and perhaps allowing themselves to be heavily dependent on a colourful solo ministry; or again perhaps the church of the suburbs or small market town which successfully focuses much of the community's life and unconsciously celebrates the virtues of intellectual confidence and being moderately successfully middle class.

Our different churches are in so many ways unique because of the subtly different forces exerted upon them, so that no one should waste time trying to tell anyone else exactly what they ought to be doing. This book has emerged out of my own urgent need to discover ways forward for mission and ministry in the particular parish where ten years ago I was instituted as vicar. It is my hope that this analysis of some of the issues in the light of my own experience may be illuminative for others besides myself, or may at least stimulate them to find alternative avenues that make sense of their own situation. This is not intended as a blueprint or detailed strategy for parish ministry in general; the autobiographical references are offered in a spirit of humility, as an attempt to guard against indulging in mere fantasy. I am convinced that experience-based theological reflection can be very helpful to others facing the same problems. Rather than developing in a line towards a high point of growth, the life of most churches over a period of time has a mixture of helpful and unhelpful experiences through which the Spirit guides them if they are listening. The hope is that the good experiences will outweigh the unfortunate ones.

However, I do not believe this can be left to chance. If we have a vision about something, it will never come to fruition unless we work with others, often on very minute details, to ensure that the vision begins to interact with ordinary day-to-day affairs. Whereas good structures in the church have no guarantee of bringing about renewal, poor structures which are not filled with a vision of what at its best the church could be, do not hold out much hope. It is painful, in analysing the churches' effectiveness, to have to make judgements about the past. Inevitably, however, every generation has a mixture of thankfulness for what it perceives as faithfulness handed on, and of rejection of what now seems anachronistic and diminishing. It is being able to throw away what holds us back that requires the greatest insight and courage.

The parish of St Wilfrid's, Halton, in East Leeds, where I worked until recently, is balanced on the edge of the inner city, with only a few aspirations to belonging to the suburbs. The area rapidly changed from being open moorland with scattered farms, quarries and mines, when earlier this century slum-clearance rehoused communities from the forests of red brick back-to-backs of the inner city, and more building land was needed for both council and modest owner-occupied housing. A large council estate has, in common with those of other cities, countless examples of deprivation and inadequacy. The entire area is residential. The bank closed through lack of interest but there are numerous small shops and estate agents' offices. Just recently a new supermarket and library have added to local amenities, built on land that has been a local eyesore for years. The population is almost exclusively white. The exceptions are a minority of West Indians and the Asian and Chinese shopkeepers. There is no real sense of the parish being a definite place that exists as a community with an identity. Rather it feels like a collection of half a dozen adjacent blocks of housing developments in which a number of community groups make bids for active allegiance: social clubs, old people's clubs, pubs, tenants' associations and churches. The church building itself, framed by poplar trees, is set on a

17

terrace high on a steep hill overlooking the City of Leeds. Designed by Randall Wells and completed in 1939 for the princely sum of £9,000, the church is a spacious, light and airy building with breath-taking sweeps in the roof interior. Large, confident transepts are matched by a large apse at the East end. The multitude of tall clear glass windows allow incoming light to set all kinds of moods within the building, not least at night, when the street lighting casts many shadows in its orange glow. Especially when floodlit, it can be seen for miles around and is a landmark on the Leeds-York railway line. The wide view from the church door takes in the vast lines of rooftops of surrounding council estates, power station chimneys, the high arc lights of the railway sidings, and in the distance the skyline of the city centre.

Since the formal creation of the Church of England parish in 1937, four incumbents, together with a number of assistant priests, have made their own decisively different contributions and have stimulated lively but contrasting models of the Church. Ian Pettit, during World War 2, offered a celibate, warm and traditional Anglo-Catholic style of ministry, giving comfort to many at a time of great crisis. He used his sense of humour, his open humanity, teaching ability and musical talents, sharing the people's life as air raid warden and as Saturday night pianist at the local pub. Consequently, as well as building up a eucharistic congregation, he also attracted a huge crowd for Sunday evensong.

The second, Ernie Southcott, along with other leaders in the Parish and People Movement in the 1940s and '50s, expended a great deal of thought and energy in restoring the eucharist to a central place in the worship of the Church of England, and to developing the practical details of its celebration. He will long be remembered for regular 5 a.m. house-communions on the council estate before people went to work in the city, for his efforts to teach parents what they were about in bringing children for baptism (often baptizing

18

as many as sixteen infants at a quarterly service), for experimenting with the physical way in which people share in worship, but chiefly for his largeness of physique and attractive personality.

The third incumbent, Kenneth Stapleton, also stayed a long time and became well loved for his traditional style of ministry: visiting, caring and with a deeply spiritual presence among the people. It was clear to him as he retired, and graciously handed over the reins to me, that the demands of mission, of theology and of the mood of society would require radical sea changes in parish life and liturgy, and that everyone would experience some pain in the process. When the bishop appointed me in 1978 it seemed that I was inheriting a going concern, a typical group of Church of England parishioners, mostly middle-aged and beyond, with a few children and young people.

I arrived with eight years' experience of very traditional ordained ministry, and with an optimism created partly by the memory of those distinguished ministries to which I knew I was a successor. Previously I had been a curate in Adel in northwest Leeds, which gave me many insights into the lives of young people in the church; then for five years I was Minor Canon and Succentor at Ripon Cathedral, which was largely a pastoral ministry to the congregation and to the surrounding villages, though there were opportunities for large-scale drama and through hosting various diocesan festivals.

It is surprising that newly-appointed parish priests do not quickly end up in a state of paralysis. I remember the burden of the sudden exposure to bearing final responsibility for an enormous building, to caring for thousands of people in rows of faceless houses and high-rise flats, and for guiding the church-going congregation through another phase of its history. I suppose God's grace, a sense of humour and a natural optimism go a long way. After all, common sense dictates that, however large geographically the parish might be, a priest will end up communicating with roughly the same number of people: if he is lucky, a couple of hundred, though the potential for the church's contact with the parish will be quite different if other members can be mobilized for ministry locally. St Wilfrid's congregation came from a great number of different backgrounds, from Four-Square Gospel through extreme Anglo-Catholic to lapsed Roman Catholic, but all alike were thoroughly accustomed both to being totally dependent on the priest and also to being quite detached and critical – usually in private, rather than at meetings.

I am sorry to say that in one sense this book is not the record of successful local ecumenical co-operation, though in another it is, because our congregation was prepared to listen to ideas and use resources from many different churches as they seemed appropriate, without being too concerned about the label attached to them. The parish I was appointed to had friendly relations with the Methodists and United Reformed Church, though with no powerful corporate plans, and was largely ignored as "not a church" by the Irish missionary order at the neighbouring Roman Catholic church. Like many others, that had its work cut out simply to perform an ultra-traditional routine ministry to schools and congregation, though as I write I am aware that the appointment of a new Roman Catholic priest has led to a quick thawing of the relationship. There was no history either of adjacent Anglican parishes engaging co-operatively together.

I soon discovered that a tiny inner core of laity with some experience of management at work were accustomed to advising and supporting the clergy, but everyone was naturally anxious at the appointment of a relatively young incumbent. They asked themselves, quite reasonably, "How long will he stay? Is it worth adapting to new ways only to have them reversed at a later date by someone else? Can we trust the ideas of someone so young?" I think we all found that slow motion, the waiting, sizing each other up, extremely painful. As a curate I was used to being able to pass the buck and to being spoiled by the elderly members of the congregation. Now as someone with a good deal of responsibility and power it came as a shock to meet a certain coolness, not to say downright suspicion. How should I proceed? I was determined not to be caught in the trap in which I had observed so many other parish priests. So often they seemed to have no strategy at all in their attempt to cope with everyone's expectations and demands, to be like a single champion holding up a shield to fend off a rain of spears from every direction. The new incumbent taking up his responsibilities could be likened to one inheriting a half-sunk boat, wondering whether he will have the capability to raise and float it, or whether it will finally come to rest on the sea bed.

My inspiration came from several years of constant interest in the theology of Vatican 2 and the ecumenical developments flowing from it. In particular I was led to look for a more vigorous and positive expectation of the Church as the People of God. Somehow I was hoping to learn to become a parish priest *from within* a Christian community, a community made aware of its unity in a common baptism through the Word of God and centred on eucharistic communion. What seemed to me to be new, exciting and releasing in Vatican 2 theology was the insight that the participation of each individual Christian and that of the bishop with his priests and deacons are different but complementary: they are equally responsible. So I came to the parish with a rather naïve vision of the possibility of seeing people not as problems but as resources, and helping every willing person to discover the gifts specifically given to them by God for ministry both within the church and the wider community.

Soon I came to recognize how much the Church of

England, like all large institutions, can play havoc with people's ideas and very lives by the radical changes of style imposed autocratically by successive decades of contrasting methods of leadership. I was determined from the start to try to become *one of the community*, not to impose ideas but to try to give people's lives and state of faith as much dignity and positive reinforcement as possible. I was keen to bring to birth a church that was not *for* the people but *of* the people. In order to get to know people better, to affirm the importance of their job and to understand a city life completely foreign to me as a countryman, I spent some time going with members of the congregation to their places of work. In some ways I had had a very protected life, moving directly through school to university, to theological college, and so into the parochial ministry. Yet despite a preoccupation for years with the demands of being educated in one of the earliest Grammar Schools to go comprehensive, living on a council estate with the economic and personal hazards of being brought up by just one parent had given me more first-hand insights into day-to-day working class life than many other clergy had. Further, to make ends meet I had worked for short periods at a variety of jobs – selling manure off a farm cart, delivering on the Christmas postal round, as a painter at an engineering site making parts for power stations, twelve-hour shifts on the hopping stage at a local brewery with free drinks thrown in several times a day, and as the lowest form of clerical life in the British Library.

Now I felt it important to spend some time with members of the congregation at their varied though often repetitive daily work. I went to work with John (who now has emphysema) as he cleared out the ash below iron foundry furnaces, with the air opaque with dust; with George (who has since died in his fifties) as he represented his firm by racing round the national motorway system; with Ian, who made bottles to contain a well-known brand of gin; with

Marilyn, who was in charge of patient records at the largest teaching hospital in Europe; with Margaret, who struggled to find jobs for the unemployed at the Job Centre; with Richard as he adjusted from being the buyer at an engineering firm to devotion to the homeless with the Church Housing Association; and with Derek who took me from my bed early in the morning to buy fruit and vegetables in the wholesale market and fitted me out with a white coat to sell cherries and strawberries in Leeds market.

This process confirmed my suspicion that the Church is sitting on and repressing a completely untapped field of talent and potential ministry which somehow has to be released. I found that urban church community to be full of people who had bypassed a lot of formal education but who had great intelligence and gifts of leadership and dogged perseverance, love and compassion, and whose faith had been tested in the crucible of real poverty of various kinds. After all, if a woman can run a school kitchen, with all its budgeting, menu-planning and staff management, combined with being a mother and housewife and keeping an eye on grandma, she's quite capable of chairing a social committee or of teaching in a confirmation group. Although it won't do for the church merely to overburden her, or for her to seek the community's or God's approval by taking on too much. So many people who are holding down responsible jobs in administration, in managing a number of fellow staff, in meeting unemployed people face to face every day, have so much to contribute to the total ministry of the parish, so long as this slogan is not forgotten: **If everyone does a little, no one need be overburdened**. Though, as many parish priests say, it's one thing to mobilize, say, thirty members of a congregation of between 100 and 150, but quite another to help the rest to a similar point of commitment. The point I am making here is that clergy with middle-class backgrounds and education should take with more seriousness the unsung skills of many parishioners. I remember with some glee one visiting priest being somewhat taken aback when he learned from a member of our congregation whether in his job he had responsibility for anyone else. Without batting an eyelid, Bill, who in his thirties had come up through the ranks in the county ambulance brigade, replied, "About eight hundred". Or again, if a market stall holder can commit himself to buying £1,000 worth of soft fruits at 6 a.m. knowing he must sell them before they go bad, there is no limit to what he and many others could contribute to the church's life both internally and in its total service to the world.

Further, I believe we should only encourage people to be the church in ways that take account of their own local culture. Christianity can only become an incarnated and authentic way of living when it builds upon and makes sense of ordinary life, here and now. Although any culture must stand under the judgement of Christ, the Kingdom that the Church must proclaim is to be worked for on earth, as in heaven. This means that the Christian community should not be allowed to become a shelter from the storm, a place of security or respectability in which to escape the dreariness and pain of human responsibilities and relationships. As Edward Schillebeeckx writes:

> The Gospel of Jesus Christ is ultimately concerned with the messianic preparation of *OUR WORLD* [my italics] to become the Kingdom of God.
>
> *Jesus in our Western Culture*

In what follows I want to put forward ideas which, if applied appropriately in differing situations, could permit laity and clergy together to build up attractive and growing local church communities with the desire and the confidence to listen to the real questions that are of concern to the society in which we are set. I recognize that many country parishes could lose heart rather than be encouraged by what I write here. But although I would support to the death their right to worship very locally, whether in church or school or home, my hope would be that they would begin to co-operate more between villages and across parish boundaries.

To begin, we need to make a brief excursion into recent theological thinking about the nature of the Church. All too often the Church, both at national and local levels, reaches policy decisions by working round to what is possible, given the people and the situation. Whilst accepting where people are, both church-goers of varying degrees of commitment and the vast numbers who are alienated or apathetic, I make a plea for ordering the life of the Church so that it more accurately reflects our understanding of our relationship with God and with one another. And rather than being a cry for individualism, where a single church leader or pressure group imposes their personal vision on everyone else, I want to open up the possibilities of whole communities exploring together the nature of their beliefs and therefore discovering together an appropriate local style for the church.

# 2

# In Tune with the Apostles

The weight of ecumenical scholarly research today suggests that the scriptures and other documents from the early centuries of church history offer no certainty about the origins of ordained ministry, except that there was a group of messengers whom Jesus himself called into a life of companionship and whom he sent out in the power of the Holy Spirit to make all people his disciples. Increasingly freed from denominational bias, scholars have written at length on how the earliest communities inherited the spirit of companionship inaugurated by Jesus, when he taught his disciples to recognize their responsibility for carrying on his own commitment to preaching about bringing forward the claims of the Kingdom of God. The gospel writers stress a "brotherliness" (Matthew 5:22–24, 43–47; 7:3–5; 18:15; 23:8) and service (Mark 9:33–35; 10:35–45) which must be regarded as more than teaching to be handed on to new disciples, but also as an essential strand within the Church's earliest way of living. I am aware that increasingly many people feel a dissatisfaction about the use of certain words which have come to be seen as unnecessarily divisive. The word "brother" is an example of how it can no longer be assumed that male terms and pronouns can speak for *all* people. I have tried to be sensitive to this throughout this book.

In those first years of the Church's existence, leaders were called and commissioned to leadership within a Christian community essentially because of the acknowledged existence of their gifts of the Spirit and their recognized participation in the community's keeping of and witnessing to the faith. Locally accepted leadership, allowing Christ's own authority given to the Church to be brought to bear, was not mere administration, nor was it based on formally defined functions. The reality of prior involvement in Christ's own mission displayed in a life of personal faith and commitment to evangelism had to be an established fact before anyone was appointed a leader within a community. A key New Testament description of Jesus' ministry, and therefore that of the Church's leaders, is "servant", meaning literally to be at the disposal of those who are sitting at table and to fulfil their needs. St Mark's "if anyone wants to be first, he must make himself last of all and servant of all" (9:35) sums up the transference from Jesus to every Christian in his service, of the essential quality of being available to all. Paul's letters include catalogues of ministries to be found in the first-century Christian communities: apostles, prophets, teachers, miracle workers, leaders, those providing support, speakers in tongues, administrators, interpreters. Clearly the expectation was that through the dedicated service of its members, according to their gifts, a community would be built up and sustained by Christ. When Paul speaks about the Spirit at work in the Church, and the gifts made available in the Christian community, he is not referring to invisible or private possessions belonging to key individuals. It is the Holy Spirit who has possession of the Church and its leaders, and not the other way round.

The majority of scholars agree that to be a minister is to be at the unconditional service of all humanity in the power of the Holy Spirit. Through Jesus, God has offered *all* people a way to fulfil their potential by responding to his love in co-operation, mutual trust and service. The task of ordained Christian ministry, therefore, was seen from the early days of the Church as one of providing help through preaching, community leadership, example of discipleship, imaginative worship, prayer and pastoral sensitivity, and of supporting men and women in their task of building up communities of love. Ministry was intended to build up such a Church, not for its own benefit, but to reveal in its life and concerns the advance of God's Kingdom. For too long now the Church has been defined as that which the clergy are thinking, saying and doing. However, our renewed understanding of Christian origins reveals the Church as a community containing the seeds of an essential ministry, rather than as a ministry in search of a Church to minister to. The notion of apostleship can therefore no longer be restricted to the clergy, as if they alone inherit the task of carrying on the programme of Jesus. All the baptized should therefore be regarded as ambassadors and heralds of the Good News. Instead of the laity regarding themselves as called from time to time to "help" the clergy, exercising authority delegated from them, the truth is quite the opposite. The clergy exist to assist all God's people, the "laity" (themselves included), to become the Church more and more effectively.

The Christian community needs to be recognized as that specific place where Jesus' vision of God's Kingdom is remembered and fostered, as the unconditional guarantee of the passionate dedication of God to human salvation. Down the centuries, as the source of grace to enable its faithfulness to Jesus' task, the heart of this community's life has been the regular and careful celebration of the eucharist. But to guard against adopting too narrow a definition of the Church there need to be recognized at least these three particular elements:

1. The proclamation of the Gospel of Jesus and the provision of the sacraments.
2. A sense of belonging to one another by baptism into the Church through the power of the Holy Spirit.
3. As in the life of Jesus himself, a commitment to service both within the brotherhood and sisterhood of the Church and indeed among all men and women.

Like Jesus himself in his earthly ministry, the Church is called to reveal God's cause in all its fullness rather than merely to serve its own ends or live to itself, in isolation from the secular world. It is fair to say that most of the time the Church fails to reveal God's hopes for all humanity and so forfeits its claim to be regarded as "the Church". Within this context a number of fundamental points about the nature or the role of ordained ministry in the Church become ever clearer. Each baptized person has a vocation within the local church, so that although ordained leadership is essential to guide and direct everyone it must never step in and usurp the rightful ministry of another. Since the Second Vatican Council in the 1960s, many writers have applied the notion of "collegiality" – sharing ministry among equals – to the contemporary life of the Church. Notably, Cardinal Suenens writes:

The fundamental role of the leader is to make collegiality possible. The role of the one in charge is not that of making a "personal" decision after taking the advice of others into account. For in that case it would still be "his" decision. His role is rather to make it possible, in so far as depends upon him, for there to be a common decision which commits each member to the decision . . . A true leader, ultimately responsible for the pastoral work of a locale, will find his place when he has succeeded in helping the others to find theirs.

Léon Joseph Suenens,
*Coresponsibility in the Church,* 1968

We need to work towards the pattern of church leadership emerging from recent theological writing; a team of ministers both ordained and lay, men and women, with a decreasing interest in an exact or uniform distinction between so-called official and unofficial ministry in the life of the community. The true Christian tradition has never allowed a fundamental distinction to be drawn between leader and led in terms of **status**; rather it has spoken of a specific and sacramental **function** of the ordained ministry to lead and preside over the community **from within**. It has been a natural reaction to ask whether or not the rediscovery of the ministry of all the baptized does not in fact do away with the need of all the baptized for the specific ministry of the ordained priest. Serving God as I do within the Church of England, I am well aware of how integral, at least in principle, are the threefold ministry of deacon, priest and bishop. As the Advisory Council for the Church's Ministry says in a recent report:

as it proclaims and realizes God's creative and redemptive activity, the Church of England is

30

*committed therefore to a Ministry of the whole People of God* and within that to an *ordained ministry*.

Education for the Church's Ministry,
ACCM Occasional Paper 22, January 1987

I believe that if we did not have ordained ministers provided by the wider Church, they would inevitably have to be invented and raised up locally to guide and lead their brothers and sisters. For God's call to ordained ministry is more than the mere management of an organization; and the involvement of laity in church ministry increases rather than reduces the role required of priests.

Just as the Church's message is more than words, and should reveal itself to the world in a practical model of obedience to the original relationship of "servant" between Christ and his disciples, so the priest is called to stand physically at the crossroads or focal point of his community as an examplar, an icon, a vulnerable, crucified figure, a stimulus towards and a mirror of Christ's own exacting Kingdom demands. For its own stable existence and for the sake of the world, the Church has to ensure that it is maintained in its apostolic character. It is vital that the local church has a minister or ministerial team whose special serving task is to maintain it in its apostolic character and task.

In the Church's tradition, "apostolic succession" has often been a phrase favoured by those who seek a guarantee of the authenticity of both church and minister. Probably in earlier, more innocent, times, before the benefits of modern scientific research were made available, the historical or physical nature of "apostolic succession" could be seriously regarded as a physical reality, an unbroken chain of bishops succeeding one to another and back ultimately to the apostles themselves. Although I do not think it is possible to understand "apostolic succession" in such a literal way, as a vital theological defence mechanism, it remains an essential part of the Church's existence. Modern writers have rediscovered the ancient principle of the right of local church communities to leadership precisely in order to safeguard the Church's origins and identity as the community of Jesus, whose mission is to keep alive in the world his unique vision of God and God's Kingdom. In the search for a completely apostolic Church we need today to abandon the understanding of apostolicity as the characteristic of bishops alone, as the successors of the twelve. The apostles were sent out to perform a task, not singly, but as a community. As Leonardo Boff, the Liberation Theologian from Brazil, expresses it:

> The first twelve remain those who deciphered the mystery of Jesus as the incarnated Son of God. We are tied to this apostolic faith and its teaching through the founding texts and the living memory of the communities of faith. Because of their function as translators and "decipherers", the apostles became the co-ordinators of those communities. Therefore, all who exercise this function of co-ordination are successors of the apostles.
>
> *Church in Charism and Power*

To be "apostolic" means that the whole church, aided by its ministry of co-ordination and "deciphering", must be seen to be a community living radically as servants of Christ, in and for the world, constantly asking the question: "If that's what Jesus and the apostles were saying and doing, what should *we* be saying and doing?" The Church needs, therefore, to be daily placing its life under the judgement of the word of Jesus

Christ, present through his Spirit to his community today. The ordained minister needs to be one chosen because he or she has the gifts, resources and wisdom constantly to represent the mind of Christ in the church, as it were holding up a mirror of the Gospel to the congregation and asking, "Are we a true community of Jesus?" So the chief service of the church leader is that of maintaining a Christian community true to the heart of Jesus and his message, in whatever circumstances and society it finds itself. In the concise language of the ACCM occasional paper 22 (January 1987):

> The ministry of the church is a *corporate one* in the church's task, but the ordained minister, *recognizing the activity of God in and for this corporate ministry*, represents it to the members of the church, focuses and collects it in a co-ordinated pattern and distributes it in the service of God's work in the world. But this work is achieved only in so far as the community of the church recognizes, trusts and sustains the ordained minister in the faith, integrity, hope, vision and love by which he or she recognizes the activity of God in it. Corporate and ordained ministry therefore animate each other, each focusing the activity of God – the work of the Holy Spirit – in the other; each therefore "brings the other to be" in the way which God's mission in the world requires. They are interanimative in the church's performance of its task, and therefore in its being.

From the earliest days ministers grew up within Christian communities so that they might be developed and nourished.

Ministers were centred not so much on the eucharist but on providing for the needs of God's People. As Schillebeeckx has written:

> Throughout the development of Ministry in the New Testament one striking fact is that Ministry did not develop from and around the eucharist or the liturgy, but from the building up of the apostolic community.
>
> *The Church with a Human Face*, SCM, 1985

Although the New Testament does not unequivocally equate the one presiding at the eucharistic celebration with the leader of the local church, the general conception seems to be that a person regarded as competent to lead the church in a general way is most likely to be competent to preside at the eucharist. Such a view is well supported by the insight that the celebration of the Lord's Supper lies at the heart of Church's life, to proclaim reconciliation in Christ and to reveal his love in the continuing mission of the Christian community. The Church's central act of worship, the eucharist, is the memorial of the act of reconciliation and the sacrament that allows its members to fulfil their mission. So it is right that the one who has oversight in the local community and is the true focus of its unity should be president when the eucharist is celebrated.

The Church can only be said truly to exist in so far as it is constantly re-identifying itself as the community of Jesus, ultimately concerned for God's cause, the salvation of humankind. In 1 Corinthians 11:23 Paul describes the eucharist as a tradition from the Lord himself, not from the apostles. Jesus promises to give himself to the church through the eucharist and it follows, therefore, that the eucharist must be the point at which the Church is most fully itself, the moment when the renewal of identity and recommitment to being God's people takes place. Because of this relationship between the eucharistic celebration and the essence of what it means to be the Church, it is not surprising to find that theological tradition has so closely linked Ministry, Eucharist and the Church:

> Reconciled in the eucharist, the members of the body of Christ are called to be servants of reconciliation among men and women, and witnesses of the joy of resurrection. As Jesus went out to publicans and sinners and had table-fellowship with them during his earthly ministry, so Christians are called in the eucharist to be in solidarity with the outcast and to become signs of the love of Christ, who lived and sacrificed himself for all and now gives himself in the eucharist.
>
> The *Lima Text*, 1982

In this brief summary of trends in theological speculation about the nature of the Church and its ministry we have arrived at a vision of a eucharistically centred local church community. In such a church every baptized person is helped by the president and team of leaders to discover and develop their own particular gifts for ministry, either within the church itself or, most likely and essentially, in the wider world of family, work, school and neighbourhood. The one who draws together the community is also charged with maintaining the common life in faithfulness to the Kingdom preached by Jesus. In the spirit of service offered typically by Mark 10:45, he must offer to every person the possibility of repentance, forgiveness and an alternative way of living, and as such is the obvious person to be presiding when the eucharist is celebrated. Is this a realistic vision for the church we belong to? Is some of this just make-believe, or does it speak in any way to the reality we know? Does it offer a helpful springboard for designing a local church strategy? I believe it does, but not without some difficulty. In the following chapter we shall examine some of the very ways in which church life, as most of us experience it, stubbornly refuses to fit the neat categories of theological theory.

# 3

# A Strong Centre but Weak Boundaries

I know how much some Church of England leaders fear that the present concern to build up a committed worshipping group will cut off many who have traditionally had an ambivalent relationship with the Church. But it need not be a matter of making a choice between a gathered and an established church. It seems to me that what we should be presenting is a Church that lives in the dynamic of immersion and dispersion. On the one hand, to be authentically the Church it needs a vibrant, joyful focus, centred on breaking the Word of God and the bread of the eucharist. On the other hand, a congregation needs to have a vision of itself as being called in hundreds of ways to be dispersed in mission and ministry in every-day situations. That constant rhythm, like the ebb and flow of the sea, immersion and dispersion, is the model of the apostolic church. Many church people believe passionately in the dispersion aspect, trying hard to be truthful, concerned, neighbourly and in so many ways living the life of God's Kingdom. However, they forget that the faith that is a response to the life, death and resurrection of Jesus Christ is a life of grace. God's mercy is a free gift, and the immersion aspect of discipleship is therefore primary. We have no alternative, therefore, but to promote a vision of the Church where first and foremost Christian people are fed, nourished, made hopeful and experience reconciliation with God and with each other. It is precisely because so many people have sampled church worship and life but have not as a consequence been brought face to face with God, that they have rejected the Christianity of the mainline churches.

No alert or travelling parish can survive for long without facing up to the vexed question of baptism policy. There are no easy answers, and it may be that just living with the messiness and ambivalence is part of the answer for the time being. It's one thing for a parish like Halton, with thirty-five baptism requests a year, to be quite positive about all of them; a parish with a hundred or considerably more can be tempted to offer little challenge. Only recently I heard of a parish with a heavy burden of baptisms deciding to have a free and easy attitude to one part of the parish but a more demanding one to another, where people seemed to have more potential for making a disciplined response. Yet one can immediately see the flaws in 'hat, as it once again sees the Church writing off the less articulate and organized members of society. Indeed it may well be that the very people who have least going for them in terms of this world's wealth and the status that education brings in our society, have the greatest potential for response to Christ if we can only communicate ideas and love in terms that can be understood.

The following story is typical of the way in which the Church struggles between the two poles of saying that baptism marks, however potentially, the start of Christian pilgrimage, with all its pains and pleasures, and that the church is concerned for every human being as loved by God, as having potential for wholeness, with a real desire to help a family celebrate the importance to them of the birth of a new child.

In the early stages of working out a parish policy, we arranged that at least one member of the congregation would support the vicar in meeting with couples who came for baptism preparation. Two hours before one such meeting with a family to discuss their baby's baptism, I excused an obviously tired lay member of our baptism preparation team from taking part: "There's only one to see and some of the family are regularly at church." Later I welcomed the small group into church and we sat down together in the nave. Although we have been working towards a more developed, caring and teaching ministry for the parents of children to be baptized, in that situation I knew that all I could offer was a welcome and a very superficial discussion of the ideas and words of the service. Usually on such occasions the non-church-going members of the party will say as little as possible, and bear themselves with a benign tolerance to the priest's inevitable spiel. "Yes, vicar, no vicar, three bags full. Whatever you say. All we want is the baby done." But on this occasion it was to take a different course. There was no hint of forcefulness in my initial remarks. So many previous occasions like that had passed without incident, indeed in a spirit of mutual generosity. Where there is lack of awareness of Christian teaching or of faith, I had always mentally covered the situation by such consolation as "Remember, Jesus is always generous with his gifts" or "Too often we ascribe to Jesus a strictness that he would not own".

The trouble began when I pointed out the absurdity of three godparents, none of whom prayed, or worshipped, or lived by trust in God. This was no problem, I was informed by the hitherto silent father, who assured me that the entire purpose of having godparents was that they should attend to the child's well-being in the unfortunate case of the parents' early death. My remonstrance to this was quickly met by the father's open admission that he had no belief in God whatsoever, that the Church in no way deserved to be taken seriously and that the baptism was "a bloody waste of time". "We're only sitting here now", he said, "for the wife's sake." He rose to his feet, marched the length of the nave and banged the church door behind him, leaving us in embarrassed silence. When I reflected with the others that his outspokenness probably mirrored the true but repressed position of many others in similar situations, they agreed and asked to be looked on generously for their frankness. The pastor in me was determined that for the mother's sake her child should be baptized, but on the Sunday morning during the service I was forced to recognize, with the father missing, grandparents anxious to placate me if necessary, and the godparents speaking out their answers as if at their own ordination, that there is much amiss.

This example illustrates some of the more complex and aggressive encounters between church communities and those who feel they should be able to have their baby baptized as of right, with no questions asked. In fact I know of a good number of couples who, sensing even the mildest challenging of this right, rather than risk confrontation or inconvenience, have persuaded another priest to be generous to them. Our parish's policy was never aggressive and we never ever refused baptism, though a small minority of parents decided not to proceed if even the simplest preparation was expected.

However, I can also think of many young couples whom I married, and who then returned with joy for me to baptize their baby. To have refused would have been plainly inconsistent with all that the Church of England tries to be. A typical example of such a couple shows them regularly at church for weeks before the baptism, with lots of people cuddling the baby. They would go conscientiously through the preparation until the day itself, when they would exhibit a great sense of celebration and fun, demand a photograph of the priest holding the baby at the font, and invite the clergy to drinks at the house afterwards. The fact that they did not continue to come to church at that time need not be an indication that their hearts had not been touched, that they had not glimpsed something of the God in whom the church community profess their faith.

There is a huge section of the population that puts "C of E" on the form when entering hospital, but does not regard this normally as making any particular demands. Within those congregations that conscientiously attempt to prepare the families and baptize children as a rule at the parish eucharist or other public service, enormous tensions can arise. Regular worshippers may say,

> "Why do we have to put up with all these people coming month after month, who have no intention of keeping the promises, who talk all the way through the service, sometimes have to be requested not to smoke in church, perhaps leave at the peace, rarely come to coffee afterwards and who are never seen again?"

There is genuine hurt here among faithful worshippers who have a deep reverence for Christ's presence in the church and sacraments, and for whom the parish communion epitomizes their basic experience of what the Church is all about. Why, they ask, should baptism appear to mean one thing for me and something else for you? The committing phrases of the Alternative Service Book, "I repent of my sins", "I turn to Christ", do not seem to support such a distinction. The temptation, in an attempt to protect the sacrament from exploitation, is for church councils to adopt extremely vigorous policies towards parents who ask for their children to be baptized without any commitment to the Church as a believing community. However, attractive as this may be, such confrontation by the inner core gives off uncontrollable negative signals to the community at large and never seems to lead to the growth of the Church.

It was my experience in urban parish life that whilst there is plenty of good will towards the Church among the community at large, and gratitude and respect for pastoral visits at times of crisis, there is a chasm fixed between those who belong in earnest, and those whose families for generations have kept their distance and who just go along for particular events. But thankfully God does not see his world through the windows of church leaders. Those who bring babies for baptism are after all a tiny minority of the total number of families, and so the trouble they take in seeking out baptism from strange people, probably in culturally threatening situations, has to be treated with great respect.

You can see how families come to a baptism with an unarticulated idea, maybe even second-hand from grandma, that they are engaging in something holy or mysterious, absolutely right for their baby and in honour of that baby's arrival. Whatever the priest says or whatever the parents and godparents are required to say publicly, the family will probably continue to "believe" what it did from the start. On the other hand, core members of the congregation and clergy feel that solemn promises are being flouted, the enormous significance of the sacrament is being ignored, and there is a frequent lack of mutual communication. The parish or deanery search for baptism policies must inevitably take up a vast amount of the Church of England's collective time, and lead to frustration because of the perennial variety of understandings of the relationship between tidy church membership and popular religious attitudes.

Not just the general lack of agreed parish baptism policies is called into question here, but the whole rationale by which certainly my own church, and maybe others too, regards itself in the context of society today. Within the congregations, of all denominations, and in society as a whole, there is a basic tension between a view of the church as a local religious agency provided by officialdom to meet the needs of occasional clients, and the belief that the Church is essentially a family, a community, a recognizable group with a corporate spirituality and task. At the heart of all the Church's anxieties and hopes for renewal this century have been haunting but unresolved questions, such as

"What is the Church?" and "Should its membership have clearly defined or deliberately vague boundaries?"

Certainly from my own experience of Urban Christianity I see little evidence of the Church holding on to a perception of itself as the soul of the nation, as if all those people out there in rows and rows of identical houses are essentially Christian but lazy or temporarily alienated from the regular life of the Church. Rather than being concerned to hold on somehow to the notion that everyone is really a Christian unless they state some new positive alternative, I am more concerned that those who do explicitly claim to be the Church should be confidently and joyfully so, but facing outwards rather than inwards. People don't in practice discover all about the Christian faith and then decide to join. Rather for one reason or another, they decide to join and then they want to find out all about it. We need to be aware of the problems people experience just observing the public image of our churches, through the witness of clergy and laity, through the media coverage and of course through occasional attendance at public worship.

As a priest I am only too aware how often, when I worship in a strange church and feel the lack of welcome, the lack of lustre or the lack of a sense of awe in the presence of God or of basic ordinary humanity, I want to run a mile, and wonder why the regulars go at all. As one committed Roman Catholic woman said to me recently, having attended a Sunday eucharist with three children in a major Anglican church, "I would never go there again!" Instead of there being a relaxed, welcoming but awesome atmosphere, where children could be allowed to be themselves, the service was clearly for adults, and the children were expected to be neither seen nor heard. Worse still, when one of the children was bored and "felt sick", and his mother had to take him out for a walk, several "helpful" stewards bore down on her and opened the door. In this way attention was embarrassingly drawn to this "emergency", which should have been regarded as natural and normal wherever children are concerned. This story is not untypical. I know of many young parents who, against their better judgement, have stayed away from church for several years rather than run the gauntlet week by week of children restless, through boredom and lack of involvement, painfully scrutinized by older parishioners whose own children probably went to Sunday School rather than church, and who, if they did go to church, certainly never attempted a four-minute mile across the sanctuary floor. In guilt, confusion and anger, young parents vote with their feet against such a church.

I believe it may be possible to avoid head-on confrontation between congregations and families wanting their children baptized, by teaching and encouraging church members to feel a collective responsibility to be welcoming and to become more tolerant by examining the sociological factors at work between all parties concerned, and actively trying to share a different model of the Church from the inherited tradition. Looking at it like this, a team of lay people visiting, preparing and following up with no trace of the "hard sell" may help to ease the tensions. Such groups of ordinary lay people may also be able to analyse where the difference in understanding lies, accept that there are no easy answers to such a messy business, and through patience and friendliness perhaps persuade some families to move over from a vague admiration of Christianity to wanting to take a positive share in being the Church, and therefore take the first steps to finding out more about it. In recent years my experience of supporting lay people preparing families for baptism has been largely with the less confident working people of the city. If they do decide to give the Church a chance in the long term, it is very difficult to see what it is that has attracted them or triggered off a response. How much is it the personality of the vicar, pastoral care in a crisis which reveals

44

what God is like, the welcome or attractiveness of the congregation, the fact of being noticed or the centre of attention, or the attraction of church membership automatically moving one up to another socio-economic category?

The Parish and People Movement in the Church of England of the 1940s and '50s, certainly in the towns and cities, gradually established the principle that to be taken seriously as a part of the catholic church a parish needs at its centre a strong vision of participating Christian fellowship centred on sharing in the celebration of the eucharist. A.G. Herbert, of the Society of the Sacred Mission, and other contributors to the collection of essays entitled *The Parish Communion* (1937) were convinced that the Church could best be renewed by taking notice of recently discovered ecumenical insights into the early Church's practice, especially regarding the nature of the Church as a eucharistic community. Now in the 1980s the Parish Communion is an established fact of life in most parts of the Church of England, though we are a long way from local churches becoming real communities. Most so-called church communities are made up of people who do not know each other by name, and are still to a large extent led by clergy who don't really know how to be primarily a member of their community, and only its president in that context. Many lay church members choose the private spirituality of the 8 a.m. celebrations of Holy Communion, with no sermon, passing of the peace, or corporate church life, having no concept of the urgent revolution of love for which J.F. Lovel Southam hoped so passionately:

There must be a process of testing, of sifting – a "calling out" of those who are ready to be "the soul of the Church". These people will set out with their parish priest to learn to know the will of God, and to witness to that will at any cost to themselves, by translating it into action ... It is not a mere question of new methods or fresh organization; people matter more than methods, and the living Body of Christ more than any organization. The Body of Christ is created, not made; its life is dependent upon the God who gave it.

A collection of individual people, like travellers waiting on a railway platform, turn up to avail themselves of the same public service but are not a community. This in itself contains seeds of total destruction. Yet, although there are signs that increasingly Christian Community is on the agenda, it is often tempting to hanker after a uniform, all-embracing strategy for church life, but can a too neatly defined Christian community really do justice to its task of proclaiming God's Kingdom in many and diverse ways? There are many who immediately say "no". Take for example the lobby to remove the modern Lord's Prayer from our eucharist. They claim that the "proper" 1662 Prayer Book version should always be used for the sake of the security of those members of the Church who rarely attend public worship. Yet, what does this say to those who work hard at making the present-day connection with the faith of the first Apostles, and to building up a confident and mission-centred Church?

It is so easy for clergy, who put so much time and emotional energy into the institutional church for so many reasons, to convince ourselves that the Church is a community when it is actually nothing of the sort. Also, at the very time when some are wanting to rediscover the Church's corporate identity there is a prevailing attitude in society which enjoys the privacy that prosperity brings, upholds the right to private religious opinion as opposed to creed, but which is totally immersed in work, family and leisure pursuits and prefers to see the church as a chaplaincy to be dropped in on when required. In *Foolishness to the Greeks* (1986), Lesslie Newbigin has challenged the churches' collusion with the general view of Western culture, that relgion is permissible if kept strictly within the private world of opinion rather than the public arena of economics, politics and world affairs. For such church people, the second verse of the hymn "I vow to thee my country" offers an excellent creed:

> And there's another country, I've heard of long ago,
> Most dear to them that love her, most great to them
>   that know;
> We may not count her armies, we may not see her
>   King:
> Her fortress is a faithful heart, her pride is suffering;
> And soul by soul and silently her shining bounds
>   increase,
> And her ways are ways of gentleness and all her paths
>   are peace.

There have been in this century large numbers of faithful, elderly, mostly female, Church of England stalwarts. In terms of discipline they are second to none. On the coldest, foggiest day, when paths are frozen, I remember ninety-year-old Mary, who on thin and brittle legs would inch her way to Sunday mass while lesser, younger mortals would look out of the window and say "not today". Yet so many of these stalwarts were, in days gone by, well trained in personal individual spirituality. I know of Dorothy, for example, who every morning sits there at the kitchen table with her magnifying glass, poring over the Authorized Version of the gospels. They attend quiet days and retreats, and generously support "overseas mission", though often they shun new liturgies and young priests with energetic ideas, and cannot see that, important as individual piety is, we are living in a new missionary age in *this* country. The model of Church

47

which served them well must now be exchanged for another. Gently but firmly we have to restore the balance between individual and corporate spirituality.

I know from my own recent experiences as a parish priest with some pretensions to working out a vision for myself and others, how hard it is to avoid the pitfall of expecting everyone to fit into our carefully constructed theories about the Church. Within every congregation I hope we shall always recognize and respect some who are called to a deeply personal life of prayer, and who find it almost impossible to engage in general bonhomie, but as a parish priest I was always in danger of being impatient with those who slip off rather than staying for coffee. The growing emphasis on the community life of the Church provides areas of conflict for those whose spouses are not practising Christians, who have to nurse invalids at home, or who are under great pressure at work. Yet when church membership is in decline and the very existence of a congregation in an urban or rural area may be in danger, it is hard for clergy and responsible laity to take a broad general view.

Introducing the total spectrum of the themes of Jesus' preaching to those who are unfamiliar with them is a long-term process and will affect different individuals in unpredictable ways. How hard it is for any church leader to resist the temptation of speeding up the process and rushing people into full, paid-up membership of the Church, without leaving them enough room to breathe, or to make a genuine free choice. While people are being helped gently to reflect on the Kingdom of God and their relationship to it, we should not be fixing dates for their children's baptisms, nor should we be burdening them with responsibility for the Church's finances, buildings, social life and administration.

Anglican churches in some urban areas do not have a "guaranteed" existence, as they might in more socially confident places. You can imagine them in a given set of circumstances just vanishing like a cobweb, blown away through the inadequacy or insensitiveness of the clergy, the movement of population or the insularity of the type of Christianity being lived there. Painfully but with amusement I recognize something of myself in the incident of a young mother, Liz, attending such a church for the first time. After the service the vicar virtually ran down the nave to greet her before she could disappear. Here was a young, normal, attractive adult. He visited her at home the next day, within two months she was on the PCC, and within six months was on the baptism visiting team. That rate of progress in fact proved right for that person, though it was alarming and funny at the time, but for many it could be all wrong. I remember having the wit to allow newly-married John and Rosemary, having just moved into the parish, a full year of regular attendance at a weekday evening mass before encouraging them to commit themselves to Sunday worship or anything else. It paid off, as John eventually made an excellent churchwarden!

We need to bear in mind the model offered earlier this century by the Student Christian Movement, in which young people, free from the restrictions of home life, were allowed the freedom to explore spiritual paths and matters of ethics and doctrine, without the bother of formal church membership if or until it was right for them.

A representative of Zen Buddhism, speaking on the radio recently, made exactly the same point. He described how he ran a shop on very relaxed lines, where the public is encouraged to drop in, whether they buy or not. Many did, recognizing their need for stillness, peace and for a new vision of their relationship to the whole of Creation. Now as a member of a Cathedral Chapter I see how many people there are needing to place a toe tentatively into the waters of faith, without being plunged into instant commitment. Cathedral buildings, with their great spaces, allow worshippers to express their confidence and commitment as they wish.

However, in searching for a right vision for the *raison d'être* of a cathedral, we are back with the same dilemmas as a parish with regard to those who choose to make a cathedral their principal focus for worship. For how long should any individual be left to him- or herself without being challenged to further commitment? It has been possible, both in parish and cathedral, for an individual to attend an early celebration of Holy Communion or Evensong for years without meeting anyone else or hearing the Gospel preached, though this is changing with the move towards providing a sermon, however short, at most services of Holy Communion. Furthermore, the question has to be asked whether it can ever be right for a church to provide uplifting, numinous, comforting worship to any congregation without pressing the common baptismal responsibi'ity to share in mission and ministry. The answer is clearly No, but there is no space here to attempt a developed answer to this important question with particular regard to cathedrals.

There are so many people in our country who, when interviewed, claim in all seriousness to have a passionate concern for spirituality, for the Bible, for justice and peace, for family life and many other concerns that are dear to the churches at their best. Many are tired of the poor example the churches offer in doing God's will, and prefer to plough a lone furrow or to dabble in several religious institutions but owe allegiance to none. Hard as it is, with buildings to keep up and clergy to remunerate, we have as churches to try to live with this and understand why it is so.

Instead of being consumed with worry about numbers in the pews and whether the church stays open, we need to concentrate on the *quality* of the Christian community life, and whether what we may call mission looks more like an exercise in survival. How many clergy and senior laity have heard themselves saying, as they lead the visiting bishop to the vestry, "I don't know where they all are today; there are usually far more people here than this." What we probably mean is that there are familiar faces missing from church every Sunday (even when the bishop comes), because only a nucleus of people do actually attend every week, much as we prefer to believe otherwise. I used to tease the people of St Wilfrid's that they must have some secret rota, known only to themselves, so that they know on which Sundays to come in order to keep the attendance about average. Our peak attendance was always Palm Sunday. Easter Sunday and Christmas Day produced no great surge of extra people (despite compulsive advertising on notice boards and through letter boxes). In fact many elderly people go to stay with their families for Christmas and Easter, and the numbers are not counterbalanced by others choosing to spend their holidays in East Leeds.

Could it be true that churches which equate evangelism with recruiting people for intense church membership tend to attract either dependent and broken people desperate for help from any source, consciously or not, or else dissidents from the church down the road, or like-minded people from similar socio-economic brackets? There is plenty of evidence in recent writings to suggest that the churches that are growing in depth and numbers have a right balance between three aspects of Christian discipleship: prayer in all its forms, study in all its forms, and an active concern for the wider community and environment in which a local church is set. Would it not be more according to the mind of Jesus if we dared to concentrate on the quality of our church community's inner life, and worked at becoming good salt, and light that really sheds illumination?

The church that emerges from this kind of approach may not be easily recognized in comparison to the one that is fading away. It may have to part company with buildings, status and an easy moralistic answer to theological and moral dilemmas. Is our religion carrying us or are we carrying it?

Driving past so many church buildings with great spires, robbed of a neighbourhood by redevelopment, reminds me so keenly of the false trails we follow, struggling to maintain the wrong buildings in the wrong places, whilst claiming to be doing Christ's will. Some church councils say, "If only, for a change, we could have some peace from maintenance and consider those important matters of mission, worship, pastoral work, involvement of children and so on." We are all too easily the prisoners of our heritage. Or again, we hear so many people criticizing "the Church", meaning the house of bishops and the clergy, for expressing doubts about the reliability of the New Testament or matters of sexual morality. We forget that the opposite of doubt is certainty, not faith. Having faith requires that we live with questions, recognizing that new knowledge makes it impossible to have a simplistic view of the composition of the New Testament or of the constitution of human beings and our behaviour. The thinking non-Christian obviously looks for some answers from any church person, and especially from official representatives. But we must not insult her or his intelligence by assuming they imagine that life's deepest problems can be answered in terms of black or white. I know I am not alone in suspecting that, despite all our nostalgia about the glories of our past history, Christianity has never really been a popular mass movement, understood and joyfully embraced by the majority. I'm not suggesting that mission and evangelism are not important, nor am I wanting deliberately to be cynical about the past, but in discovering for ourselves in our time a vision of faith, rather than certainty, to which we can be true, let's not get misled into wanting a church that is a human success story. The Church is called primarily to be the servant of the God who in the Resurrection set his seal of approval on his portrait as drawn uniquely in the life, teaching, suffering and death of Jesus. Can we dare to leave off fighting to create a Church that is strong, packed to the doors, eloquent and confident, as an irrelevance which no one needs, least of all the God who revealed himself most starkly in the figure of the one who was crucified outside the city wall?

# 4

# Leading Differently

If you see the Church as a highly structured, efficient society with clear goals, you will look for a leadership that is strong, confident, expert, and able to mobilize people, delegate tasks, manage groups, make clear public statements, administer and anticipate problems. In Britain earlier in this century relations between members of the Church could be very formal, with bishops deliberately keeping even their senior staff at arm's length, and members of Parochial Church Councils talking in pompous language and referring to one another as Mr Brown or Miss Jones. Even in those parishes in which Christian names have been much more readily and widely used, many of the clergy themselves have preferred the protection of being called Rector, Father or Canon.

We tell society who we think we are by the clothes we choose to wear. The great variety of clerical garb to be seen in the streets today is a reflection partly of a confusion of identity among the clergy, partly of a desire to say very firmly who we think we are, and partly to be chameleon-like in sinking into our surroundings. For example, a clergyman in a black suit with a traditional collar may well be telling himself and everyone else that, though life itself is changing beyond recognition, the faith we have inherited, the Church and the clergy have not lost their way. A clergyman in a sports jacket with patched elbows, traditional collar and perhaps a beard could well be a social radical, while the wearing of a check shirt, tie and olive green knee-length waterproof coat is a sure sign of the country priest on his way to meet the locals at the pub. I won't pursue these caricatures, but the clothes we wear in the parish give off clear signals. I know I very seldom wore a suit in Halton because in that place people of my age didn't wear formal clothes unless they worked in a bank, represented their company or were attending a great family occasion. Regularly to wear a suit there would be to say that a priest is separate and professional like a doctor, the head teacher or the manager of the supermarket. Yet of course there are many clergy who are serving in places where most people wear formal dress most of the time unless they are on holiday or taking time off. To wear a pullover and jeans in this situation could be to say that the life of the Church is a hobby for leisure time and has no connection with the world of work or public lines of communication. Some regard the cassock as the obvious alternative to avoid these pitfalls, yet I suspect that today this speaks to the general public more of eccentricity and obscurantism than of anything else. The television comedy portrayal of a bishop or priest is most successful in strikingly odd clothes like surplices and copes.

As a young parish priest, for me to attempt to offer a radically different model of church and expectations of leadership was extremely difficult. I mentioned earlier how I went to East Leeds enthused with the basic theological ideas of Vatican 2 about the Church as a co-responsible missionary body. I had a vision of the Church as a community of believers sharing a common life. Such a Church would place a stress on openness and on building up a family atmosphere in which as many strata of society as possible would feel at home. Above all in an essentially working class area I did not want people to have to part company with their culture and roots in order to live "the life of the Church". A church needs to have "psychological space" for all those it genuinely wishes to include in its membership. To become this sort of church, I recognized, would need me to be a priest with three basic characteristics:

1. I should be able to help the people become the local church through offering them a clear vision but not by exercising authority over them in a formal style.

2. Rather than operating from a position of power over a dependent group, I should need to concentrate on drawing out in as many people as possible a sense of maturity, as I shared my convictions in an open and patient way.

3. I should need not only to express these convictions in words, but be able to witness to them in my style of working within the community, as well as to articulate to the church members what they were doing and how that related to the wider Church's experience and aims.

There are Church leaders who shake their heads at such language, either preferring to put all their trust in "the ministry of the faithful pastors and teachers" (Collect of St Matthias) as referring to themselves, or else claiming there is nothing new in all this talk of shared ministry and that they have been doing it all for years. I know how uneasy some are at what they regard as the apparent reduction of priesthood to the "leadership" of Christian communities. Some believe that this approach has evacuated "priesthood" of its true significance, and find expressions like "the leadership of ordained ministry" too weak to count as true "up-front" priesthood at all. My understanding of "leadership" is as one who begins essentially as a baptized member of a Christian community, but who has been given by the bishop the responsibility of representing the Catholic Church for sharing in his own ministry of oversight, and given permission by the local congregation to "recognize", co-ordinate and distribute the ministry of others' (ACCM Occasional Paper 22, January 1987). As Alan Wilkinson, one of the "Founding Fathers" of the St Albans Diocese Ministerial Training Scheme, has written about the distinctive role given to the ordained minister:

> The priest focuses with particular clarity and representativeness what is (or ought to be) true of the life and work of the Church as a whole.
>
> *Growing into Ministry*,
> Ed. B.E.E. Pettifer, p.5

This is not to say that I did not consider pastoral work important. In fact I hope that a pastoral approach undergirded all that I did as a parish priest. My predecessor had put most of his energy into visiting the able-bodied and the sick and bereaved. Soon after I arrived it was clear that I was going to be putting a lot of energy into presiding over the ministries of others, giving them vision and support. One of the older ladies, showing that she had taken notice of this, but not in a critical way, said, "I know you're not one for popping in to see us a lot, but I'm sure you'll be there when we need you". I tried to see everyone in their home at least once, but felt very strongly about a number of things concerned with visiting.

In the first place the sick, housebound, troubled and bereaved need to be cared for either by clergy or by members of the congregation. There will always be some members of the church and some for whom the church is responsible who need caring for, though who they are may vary considerably from year to year. Secondly, it is a mistake regularly to visit the hale and hearty, because this reinforces in them the image of a priest who is there to look after them rather than as one to preside over their many and varied ministries. Thirdly, housebound members of the congregation (whether temporarily or in the long term) may wish to receive communion. If this is left entirely to the clergy in a large parish it is unlikely to be possible more than once a month. However, if a small team of laity are properly prepared and supported in this work, there is no reason why people should not receive communion at home as frequently as is appropriate for them.

I recognized too that a great deal of informal visiting of the lonely and sad goes on within and around a congregation anyway, but did encourage those who wished to see their visiting as clearly representing the church to meet once a month. At these meetings we shared what was right, with respect for the natural need for confidentiality, supporting those who were finding it hard to visit difficult people. I took my share in this work, visiting the chronic housebound, teasing those "housebound" I happened to have spotted coming home on the bus out of town, listening to the often repeated stories of past hurts, spending time at parties after baptisms, weddings and funerals, and wondering what to say after responding to the usual "What a lovely church, vicar!" and "Thank you for a lovely service", containing the bitterness of feuding neighbours, drinking the health of octogenarians, sometimes arriving at the busy teaching hospital just after the patient had left for home, dropping in regularly on old people's clubs, and chairing their annual meetings and visiting the parents of members of the Guides company, sitting in silence with the young couple whose baby's death had attracted police investigation, and trying not to be too hurt when greeted at the church door with, "I'm better now, didn't you know I was poorly? You never came." Involvement in pastoral work is vital for a priest if he is to be in touch and know the congregation and the parish, but it is not appropriate for him to do it all.

In the fourth place, of course, the members of the congregation need pastoral and spiritual care while they minister to others, but this is done best in one-to-one interviews at church or somewhere other than in their home amid the rest of their family. I have devoted the whole of chapter 7 to this important task.

In the next three chapters I shall try to explain the specific elements which I identified as necessary for me to bring to life, as the parish priest's contribution to this process. It was an informal "mandate" or contract, worked out but not articulated through church committee meetings, in teaching and in just sharing a common life with those at the heart of the church community.

# 5

# Oversight of the Community

A parish needs a priest who can help it discover an over-all picture of what it is about. Many busy parishes are involved in a dizzy collection of many and very worthwhile activities, or are engaged in trying to sort out a host of people with problems. Church meetings often seem to be called to plan activities or solve problems: getting new Sunday School teachers, working out the service patterns, repairing the roof, finding people to read lessons, raising funds, or finding lifts to church for the elderly. In such a situation the priest will find he is largely concerned with seeing that these activities take place efficiently. The effectiveness of a parish may even be measured in terms of the number of successful activities it can stage. A parallel can be seen in the way we have trained clergy in theological colleges this century, examining briefly many very important and worthwhile topics in isolation: some knowledge of the Bible, liturgy, doctrine, ethics, with practical guidelines on visiting, funeral-taking, hearing confessions, concern for drug abusers and the problems of inner cities, and an introduction to children's work. Parish staff meetings too easily degenerate into who will cover which services, take which funerals, preach when, and administer communion to the housebound. In other words, much of church life is reaction to the problems and situations which are thrown up by the congregation and parish.

Although I wouldn't for a moment suggest that church life can be too tidy or unrelated to the crises which every day brings, there is a clear need to take a longer look at parish life. There is a great deal to commend the working out of a vision or goal, with aims and objectives which can be checked and measured from time to time. We could start by asking questions such as, "In what human context is our church set? What is the Church for? Where are we going? Does most of what happens here contribute to the process by which we move toward becoming what the Church should be?" The priest who takes such a view will need to do more than make sure that, with help from the laity and through a winsome personality, he sets in motion some interesting and worthwhile projects. The priest needs to have a grasp on what the goals of the Church are, and what resources are available to bring them about. He has the task of presiding over and helping the community to keep on course, pursuing those goals and, wherever necessary, adapting itself to become more and more effective.

Through my growing into presidency in the parish I came to see that the priest has the awesome responsibility of teaching and encouraging others to teach the Christian faith to all members of the congregation. It is his business to be aware of and to point to recent insights into the working of the human mind and their relevance to teaching the faith in the present generation, and to make these resources available, sometimes with the help of the wider Church. There were other members of the congregation who outshone me in teaching ability, requiring me to learn to share the teaching and preaching of the Gospel while not abdicating responsibility for it. I found I had to discover my own unique resources for patiently but persistently living out the role of president, often against the expectations of some parishioners.

I wanted to remain vulnerable and open to the congregation, indeed wanted to say, "This was your church before it was ever mine and you will be here, no doubt, after I have gone", but on the other hand I had the responsibility to keep that community in communion with the whole worldwide Church and I was aware of renewed insights which I believed all churches should be challenged by. On the one hand I wanted to affirm all that was already good in terms of the pursuit of personal wholeness and devoted pastoral care, and yet offer the possibility that there were other avenues to explore, especially involving the laity. It's all too easy to come into a new parish like a new broom and criticize all that has gone before, not recognizing the partiality of every generation's vision, including your own, though to remain too objectively critical of your present vision in the light of eternity can be paralysing. Some parishioners, for example, were not at all keen to move the church furnishings according to the insights of today, even when most of the congregation had grasped the vision and new possibilities, because in fifty years' time some new fashion would no doubt come along and it would all either have to be "reversed" or changed in some other way. Our generation seems particularly deferential to previous centuries' fashions in church lay-out, often failing to recognize just how much our old parish churches and cathedrals have been constantly changed and knocked about to serve the confident insights of succeeding schools of thought about the worship of God. To take to extreme lengths the view that our generation's vision is only partial could prevent us from ever doing anything at all.

Other members of the congregation pointed out how hard they had worked during the time of one of the former vicars, as though this allowed them to freewheel now. My response was to point out that there can be no retirement age for church members. Everyone's deepening insights are required. There may be times of more or less involvement with the formal life of the church for just about everyone, except, it seems, the clergy – though how many of us would go to church every Sunday if we weren't ordained? And, having exhorted all our parishioners to go to church on holiday, how many of us would take a quiet Sunday off under the same circumstances? I always want to stress, against the way our society operates, that a congregation needs the insights of both the quite young and the fairly old, and that if everyone does a little, no one need be over-burdened.

There is a theory that Christians learn their individual orthodoxies at a particular point in their lives, perhaps in confirmation classes or from a priest who at some stage influenced them in a powerful way. Ever afterwards, so the theory goes, we test out all other experiences of church against that orthodoxy, giving it mental marks out of ten. As a young parish priest, I found a number of confident older members of the congregation who made it clear in toughish, direct words that they knew what Christianity and church membership was all about, having learnt it from church or Father and that they were puzzled or annoyed that I should presume to teach them something different.

One country Rector I know laughs at this predicament, saying that he gets great comfort from mowing the church-yard, where he is able to chat to former parishioners, lying beneath his feet, in the full confidence that they no longer have the right to reply or obstruct his policies. Another priest who introduced a highly controversial baptism policy proudly admitted at a clergy chapter meeting that he had "got it through the Church Council on a cold wet night in January". There is also some grain of truth in the apocryphal story of an ebullient priest saying at the end of a stormy debate at Council meeting, "Now brothers and sisters, this is a difficult decision, and we shall expect all those who vote against the motion to resign". Certainly, over the years I came to see the temptation gradually to end up with a Church Council that was in general agreement with my understanding and, subtly or otherwise, to ease out any opposition. In fact there is a real sense in which those whom we may in shorthand call "traditionalists" need to be encouraged to hang on to say what they feel called to say for the sake of the total apostolicity of the Church in a particular generation, though it's hard for anyone to be always having to say "no" to things against the prevailing mood.

The problem remains, how does a clergyman and those lay people committed to moving into collaborative ministry and the kind of worship that expresses it, progress with confidence, though not at the expense of leaving everyone behind? It's rather like good practice in climbing a mountain. You can only move at the speed of the whole group. It's no use a few fit and adventurous members of the group shooting off into the clouds, leaving everyone else behind, bewildered and annoyed. Even the most entertaining and worthy of clerical initiatives in parishes with house groups, elders and so on, is only as strong, in the long term, as the extent to which it has moved slowly enough for it to be possible for the majority of the congregation to share profoundly in the praying, the planning, the over-all vision and decision taking.

But there can be real anger expressed by parishioners who may in their hearts feel powerless to defend their way of seeing church life from a new priest. I can think of ladies who in their private piety were very loving and diligent, but who, naturally enough because of their generation (both humanly and theologically), had little sense of the corporateness of the Church's worship or ministry. Those who had been brought up in Anglo-Catholic parishes to have a healthy respect for the priesthood, were especially confused to have a priest who was happy to be called "Father Robin" and to refer to the eucharist as "the mass", but who wanted a nave altar, provoked open discussion about doctrine and was happy to have women commissioned to administer the chalice. Another side to this was the dichotomy between me being friendly and pleasant, but knowing that some things had to be, slowly but inevitably, painfully changed. A number of senior lay people, I recall, would say, "If what you are proposing, for example about worship, will offend a single person, we shouldn't do it". Whilst I never felt that voting and being satisfied with narrow majorities at the Church Council was appropriate to the life of the People of God, I didn't on the other hand see that you could wait for an absolute consensus. There is an important sense in which the Council had been specifically elected to represent the congregation, and when decisions were taken it was important for them to be allowed to feel the corporate responsibility and the element of risk involved.

Regarding the difficult decision about how to make sense of the East end of the church, which was the sanctuary before the introduction of a nave altar, it was clear to me (though disappointing and surprising) the first time the Council discussed it, that there were so many anxieties about "taking axes and hammers to the Lord's house", that it should not be pursued until later. It was only after two years of teaching, discussion and experimental use of that area for weekday services, that plans were eventually drawn up and agreed without difficulty, even with the positive encouragement of regular weekday worshippers, for the imaginative development of a Lady Chapel.

I feel thrilled that it was during the interregnum, after I left the parish, that there has been sufficient confidence and vision for the money to be found and the work of creating this change to be done, mostly by members of the congregation, rather than awaiting the arrival of a new parish priest. It is a delicate balance between looking to a new priest for direction and oversight, and yet not expecting or allowing him to, as it were, mentally put up a sign saying "Under Entirely New Management". There is a point at which the local congregation have to be able to say to an incoming itinerant priest, "We have prayed and struggled to this or that insight; please, if you come to be our president, try to understand and respect where we are, and only then with great sensitivity lead us forward". In other words, the coming and going of various clergy in parishes should less and less mark out definite new chapters or completely different epochs of initiative in their history.

As part of the parish priest's unenviable role of representing in his whole life the Kingdom to the church, I often had to challenge the attitudes of committees and individual people, asking whether they were really building up the Church of Christ or something else. Sometimes individuals had to be encouraged to forgive one another, or to stop a course of action or line of conversation, or to begin to look for the best of someone else, for the sake of the local church family in which all who wish should be allowed to play an appropriate part. This part of the priest's work can be very time-consuming and easily seem like autocracy unless it is clearly seen to be based on a spiritual basis rather than on merely human confidence. Positive teaching about the nature of the Church, pastoral care and a sense of humour were of most value in my own case in discouraging people from pursuing a Christian life based on dependency on me or the curate. Eventually, after a number of years of sharing responsibility with quite a large proportion of the total congregation, I found that the basic principles began to take root, even to the extent that others began gently to check me when I failed to live up to them. I found great encouragement in the principles of the growing catechumenate movement, which sees the whole community as committed to bringing others to the faith through the total life of the local church: worship, prayer, Bible study, social life and plans for mission of many kinds. I found that half a dozen committed lay people could adapt a published training course such as Wim Saris' *Together We Communicate* and put it over in an attractive style, given the encouragement and support of the clergy on the parish staff. Liturgically there is much enouragement in the American Prayer Book Supplement, *The Book of Occasional Services* (1979), and in Peter Humfrey's *Confirmation, a Community Preparing* (1985). It was not always easy to find just the right adults for this task in Halton, but in a confident middle-class parish this would present fewer problems. As parish priest I was responsible for checking on the content of the teaching, for helping the lay teachers prepare their sessions, leading weekends away, and for helping the whole congregation to see that they were all responsible for teaching the faith to those preparing for the sacraments of baptism and confirmation and for making them part of the family, even though the specific task of teaching had been delegated to six people.

The way a parish worships on Sundays is like the tip of an iceberg: it reveals what lies beneath the surface. I believe this to be so central that I have given this a separate treatment in another chapter. The planning of worship is too important to be left to the clergy alone. In my own experience a music and worship group, containing a cross-section of the congregation and a priest, planning well ahead, can revolutionize the possibilities for worship that is popular, varied, lively and confident. The Church only exists where the eucharist is celebrated; but the dry bones of observance need to be brought alive by making worship truly a celebration where many bring together their careful contribution. There are lots of booklets around these days with ideas to set such a group going for planning vigils and what our American friends rejoice to call "para-liturgies", as well as the increasing literature generated by the Catechumenate Movement. I believe that, provided this movement can forget the complicated jargon of past centuries, it is a great source of encouragement for the future, especially because it allows congregations to show in church life the importance of *every* member in bringing others to faith.

We all need more confidence too in introducing silence and

stillness into worship and church life generally, constantly observing God in the small and simple. "Measuring lizards on the Road to Assisi" was the title of a Franciscan community retreat led by David Goodacre, in which I had the privilege of sharing. We reflected on the progress of a family making a pilgrimage to Assisi on foot. They eventually learned to go at the pace of their youngest son, who kept stopping all the time, fascinated by the lizards on the path and stooping down to measure their length with a pencil. On that same retreat we were all encouraged not to read at all, to find a simple leaf or flower in the garden and spend a lot of time examining its structure, maybe with a view to painting it later, to go slowly on walks and to observe God present in his creation and in our life now. I see this as a helpful parable for those who would engage in the painstaking building up of a collaborative Christian community with deep roots.

Judging how fast or how slowly to move the community along, and how to know when to push a new idea and when to wait is one of the most difficult tasks and cannot be done successfully unless we listen to what is being said within the community. The measure in which we as priests are really able to hear what is being said will be a reflection on how far we have been able to build up a sense of intimacy, and how much we have been prepared to be vulnerable in the way we hold ourselves before people and to have time enough to "waste". No management structures in the world can achieve this.

This style of presiding of course creates all kinds of new questions and demands a willingness to experiment and take risks. If it is to take root generally it must require a new sort of candidate for ordination, with a willingness and capacity to lead a local church with vision, enjoyment and firmness but primarily as part of a team. But perversely, such ordinands will not be forthcoming until this new model is actually experienced over a period and seen to be working effectively in parishes, so inspiring men and women to come forward to be trained to do it. It also raises questions about how men and women should be selected for ordination, and about the wisdom of training for the priesthood entirely undertaken in residential colleges, perpetuating the notion that the clergy are a race set apart.

The very professionalism encouraged by the separating off of the ordinand in training jars with the style of church that many look to see in the future. This is not to say that the selection and training of clergy should be unprofessional or lacking in care and effectiveness. I remember one priest (ordained in 1920) telling me how, staying overnight at the bishop's house, he was eventually interviewed for fifteen minutes by the hard-pressed bishop, sitting on the edge of his bath, having been so occupied during the evening that there was no other time. In the process of selection of clergy, we could note that all Methodist ministers have their vocation tested primarily in the local circuit. It is said that a prophet is not without honour, except in his own country, but certainly I believe that in the Church of England we do not allow the local congregation sufficient involvement in the selection of clergy. It looks very much like the ruling class perpetuating itself by appointing its own successors. The arguments for and against Residential and Non-Residential Training are being much aired in the circles where decisions are made by the Bishops, ACCM and the Colleges and Courses, and there are no simplistic solutions that will cover all cases.

With regard to the selection of future clergy, we should be looking closely at the candidate's willingness and ability to be primarily a church community member, rather than an individual freelance professional. Some of those recently ordained, with experience of being active lay people in parishes that encourage collaborative ministry, certainly seem to be freer from the protectiveness and separation of clergy selected and trained in previous decades. I believe that

69

the plans we make for training should allow all ordinands the opportunities for Christian fellowship, introduction to challenging theological ideas, opportunities to strengthen their spiritual life, but not at the long-term expense of separation from their family or cultural roots, or separation from local church life, the stimulus of every-day or working life, ecumenical links, and those in training for other categories of Christian ministry. Without wanting to abolish residential training altogether, because I know how much I gained from it in terms of spiritual vision, theological resources and confidence, I want to stress how much there is that is positive when on the non-residential courses men and women of all traditions can learn from one another, are still closely rooted into their parishes, families, places of work and leisure, can enjoy a common 'ife, are challenged with new ideas, and train with those whose future ministries will be complementary though quite different from their own. Can the residential courses worry less about covering so much ground and having everyone so busy and bound up with meeting deadlines, and instead reflect in their corporate lives the holistic vision required of future parish priests, with the responsibility chiefly of presiding over their communities and working in teams with one another and with Readers and others of the congregation?

We should stop kidding ourselves that any one clergyman has all the gifts; we all need to help the clergy to relax about wearing the parish as a badge of their own personalities, abilities and strengths. The Church needs to have the courage to let people make mistakes and to find out what it means to be in charge, yet not in such a way as to cramp or distort the responsibility of anyone else. There needs to be a generous give and take within the community, as if the priest is saying, "Yes, I am the one presiding, but only *from within*"; while the people generally say, "Yes, you are *within*, but you are also called to be in *charge*". This is not subordination, nor is it exactly democracy. All this is one side of the notion of "companionship" which I believe to be the most reliable peg for being sure we are saying and doing in appropriate ways *now* what the apostles were saying and doing then. It is doing to death the idea of a Church that is *for* people and is rather a Church that is *of* people, no longer a holy supermarket where you buy without commitment or love.

But while we work to make the group of people who "go to church" into a genuine community that *is* the Church, who, as the Latin root of the word "commitment" implies, "go out together" to do things, the president has to keep in mind the danger of the congregation becoming sectarian. As William Temple reminds us, "The Church is the one organization in the world that exists purely for the benefit of those who do not belong." It is perversely true that in the process of building up a local church as a close-knit group, committed to being godly and missionary – that is, the People of God as described classically in 1 Peter 2:1–10 – we run into the danger of becoming a closed and inward-looking private club. Christian community becomes very distorted indeed if it is not looking outwards or trying to become a signpost indicating in its own life the far greater vision of the right relationship that should exist between all people. It is this kind of insight that is implied when St Francis refers even to parts of the created order as brother and sister. And this is all because Jesus came to tell us in his life, death and resurrection that God's passionate cause is the wholeness of humanity and the unity and well-being of the created order.

The Apostles discovered that Jesus was the Messiah. To their amazement, the Messiah that Jesus was did not concern himself with just one favoured group within society. For Jesus' God the enemy is not some other person, but the egotistic self, one's own life (Luke 9:24). Jesus' God calls us to lose our lives for his sake and to be the willing slaves of all

(Luke 9:24). We must love our enemies radically because they are sons of the Father who makes the rain to fall on the just and on the unjust (Matthew 5:44f). "Whoever does the will of my Father is my mother, sister and brother" (Luke 14:26). The parable of the weeds in the wheat reveals that here there is no division between insiders and outsiders (Matthew 13:36–43).

As well as keeping mission at the top of the parish agenda, often with a struggle, I found that keeping ecumenism there was more difficult. Despite constant efforts to change attitudes, only a minority of any of the Halton churches seemed very committed to growing together, though occasionally we held joint services and children's festivals. No one group should pretend that it has a monopoly on salvation. A moment of light relief may be had at the expense of this victorial hymn writer extolling the Roman Catholic self-awareness of being the ark of salvation:

> Who is She that stands triumphant
> Rock in strength, upon the Rock
> Like some City crowned with turrets
> Braving storm and earth-quake shock?
>
> Empires rise and sink like billows
> Vanish and are seen no more;
> Glorious as the star of morning
> She o'erlooks the wild uproar.
>
> Hers the Kingdom, hers the sceptre,
> Fall ye nations at her feet;
> Hers the truth whose fruit is freedom
> Light her yoke, her burden sweet.
>
> Aubrey de Vere

We may smile at this arrogance but it is perpetuated still

72

between denominations, even between neighbouring parishes who refuse to collaborate but insist on going it alone. As a sequel to the David Jenkins affair a letter appeared in *The Times* newspaper by a former Anglican priest who has joined the Orthodox Church, where he confidently referred to his new spiritual home as the "one true church". Walking home from school with the children I was in conversation with the wife of the leader of a house church of an evangelical group. We were discussing our respective churches and she said, "I used to be an Anglican but my husband and I got so fed up with the divisions between the churches that we decided once and for all to start the one true united Church of Jesus Christ". And this they have done in their own front room.

I recognize that it takes a certain amount of determination, not to say recklessness, to pursue in a single-minded way this model of presidency. There will be other expectations in the mind of the parish. A survey carried out in 1977 revealed that the majority of clergy regarded their primary role as that of a pastor, whose task it is to care for those entrusted to him though in fact the system they may be expecting to operate, given the present situation, may be both impossible and inappropriate to fulfil. There have been many great priests in the twentieth century whose lives have been shining examples of the traditional servicing and solo style of ministry, accompanied by a deep sense of personal holiness. It would be wrong if there came a time when for some priests this was not their major concern. There are wise and holy priests in a few rural parishes who feel called predominantly to lives of study, prayer and moving slowly and deeply among their flock, as one Welsh poet has put it, "keeping house" for God. Such hermit-like parish priests have their small devoted congregation and are often sought out as spiritual guides. There are as many ways of being a priest and a community of Jesus as there are of climbing a mountain, and we shouldn't waste time telling others that they are on the wrong path.

However, it seems most unlikely that the quiet, self-effacing style promoting personal piety will be required of most parish priests in the immediate future. Indeed I am convinced that clergy have too many eggs in the pastoral basket. Priests who at the moment are attempting to provide front-line pastoral cover within a cluster of parishes will in fact be already spending a high proportion of their time preparing and leading worship, travelling and trying to meet fixed-point commitments in all the communities. Although I counted myself fortunate in having only one church building, I found that to have the courage to put as a priest's primary role leadership of all the ministries around him, means taking administration seriously, constantly encouraging the work of teams, groups and committees, being available to influence key situations in the wider community beyond the church, encouraging people to see that the priest needs *their* ministry to *him*, keeping regular time of silence each day, keeping abreast with reading, and providing personal spiritual guidance to those who are learning to minister in new ways. But there is little evidence on a wide scale that this is being faced up to.

Each priest in differing situations needs to give himself the opportunity, in close collaboration with the members of the church, to work out a strategy. No one model of leadership will be found that will neatly replace the outworn one of the nineteenth-century professional solicitor or doctor. We could learn something from the informal national and local networks of voluntary caring organizations or part-time leisure activities which have grown up this century and are in the main extremely successful. In particular they place a great emphasis and trust, for reasons of economy, on highly motivated volunteers. The human sciences can help us if we choose to let them. Though we all know of clergy who close their eyes, smile knowingly and switch off when the phrase "as sociologists have said" is mentioned.

Sociology helps us to ask the questions: "Do our existing methods of exercising authority really work? Are they the ones we need for the future?" A recent Open University lecture on the radio provided two contrasting models drawn from industry. On the one hand we all know the style of the tough, ruthless manager, the boss who hands down orders and must be obeyed without question or delay. Other people only have authority because he gives it to them, and he regards everyone else as raw material to be used and manipulated to achieve *his* goal. On the other hand, in extreme contrast is the motorcar co-operative. Here the key is the regular meetings of all concerned to make joint decisions about means and ends. The result is to be able to say "My friends and I have built this entire vehicle". They have as a team done something that is creative and satisfying, and the whole process is most effective. Which of these two models comes nearer to what we need in the Church?

Many of the critics of new styles of church life and ministry make the complaint that these are merely signs of a liberal church leadership desperately trying to make the faith palatable to an increasingly secular society. The accusation that the Church is conforming to the world, replacing for example in worship, the atmosphere of the Byzantine Court for that of the Company Shareholders' Meeting, does not do justice to the evidence. A more accurate assessment is more like this: whereas the total number of faithful Christians, in Europe certainly, decreases annually at a quite alarming rate, and as a consequence the numbers of candidates for the stipendiary ministry have fallen off, there are thousands and thousands of local churches in many forms where life itself is strong and growing. In those places where a flourishing and vital church prevails, a close examination reveals a body of people, professional, managerial and administrative workers, as "skilled" in their own way as the clergy who lead them, who have been given insight into the responsibility of all the baptized for promoting the Kingdom. Such places where the Church is increasing in numbers and in depth of commitment have experienced changes in clerical-laity relationships, in the style, spirituality and model of authority operative in the church. There has been a stimulating move from autocratic or hierarchical government towards an experience of mutual accountability and a spirit of consultation and shared decision-taking. There is little sign of a new springtime for the Church in so many places where under clerical domination the old structures are slowly grinding to a halt, and where there is no vision at hand to replace them. Yet perversely it is so often in these quarters that criticism is strongest of the invitation to collaborative ministry and of a challenging vision of the local church as a corporate agent of mission.

# 6

# Living at the Crossroads

As the president or overseer of the parish, the priest is one who has to learn to be the co-ordinator of the ministries he evokes in others. In this I found there are many pitfalls: relying on the same people too often, misjudging the abilities of people to carry responsibilities, allowing people to believe they carry burdens handed out by the vicar rather than themselves, because of the commission of baptism and confirmation, engaging fully in the Church's mission, to say nothing of the human sins of jealousy and dishonesty, and tiredness and depression. Especially in an urban church community that contains few of the sort of people who exercise authority at work, it is vital for the clergy to give constant encouragement when what has been achieved or proposed is worthwhile and valuable, even though it may be quite different from what we might have thought of ourselves. It requires a degree of sensitivity and true companionship to be able to achieve this without perpetuating the old ways of clerical proprietorship or patronization. The difficulties of an in-coming priest to a community of which he has no real knowledge or experience are well known. Church leaders and community workers with middle-class backgrounds often fail to recognize that there is a strong pull in working-class communities for those who "make it" to "get out", to be successful and to become middle class, and that this may often result in a sustained effort to reject the culture and environment of the district where a working-class person has grown up. It is remarkable too how these people who do move up to the lower rungs of the home-owning middle classes are tempted to lose sympathy and patience with the group of which they were recently a part. It takes a middle-class social activist to get romantic about the solidarity of the working, unemployed or under classes. Young couples who could afford to get married in Halton, almost invariably tried to move into home ownership, even if for a few years that meant moving further into the inner city until they had saved enough to move out to suburban villages. Those from the council estate who married and remained were often the truly "poor", unemployed and extremely inadequate ones. How can the Church begin to show by its acceptance and message God's love to them in a relevant way, such that they could come to see themselves as members of that Church?

How essential it is in building church communities in urban areas to have clergy who can see value in the existing culture of the area, rather than simply trying to change it.

Adrian Hastings, in his recently published *A History of English Christianity 1920–1985*, reflects on how the Church of England, with its upper-class central leadership, inevitably at the local level in cities like Leeds invites new members to better themselves socially. During this century, Hastings suggests this was partly due to the motivation of the middle-class Anglican clergy, who felt moved to change the living conditions of "the poor". By contrast, the Roman Catholic clergy have by and large been more likely to build up communities of "the poor" and support them in their suffering. I would have to say, criticizing myself among them, that I have not met many itinerant Church of England clergy who are really prepared to move at the speed of the people they serve. Indeed, whilst the present structures continue in however diminished a form, and whilst clergy continue to dominate urban communities with their own middle-class expectations and to patronize them unconsciously with single-handed "hard pressed" caring and managing, progress in building a truly local church is postponed, though perhaps we may hope the foundations are being laid.

A taxi driver who had trained for the ordained ministry in East London commented on the Church's usual lack of nerve to rely on styles of leadership other than safe middle-class ones:

> Every time we try to be leaders, every time we try to take our affairs into our own hands, we press a button inside us that tells us that we are not up to it. And so even in the process of exercising leadership, of acting out our potential, we are putting ourselves down and reinforcing our inner conviction that we just haven't got what it takes.

> *Building an Indigenous Church in East London*, Stepney Action Research Team, 1980

It is difficult for parish priests, unconsciously wearing their parishes like badges of success or effectiveness, to take the risk of allowing others (ordained or lay) to operate freely from within their own cultures.

For seven successive years in our parish in Halton we valued the experiment in Christian community living of a parish holiday, deliberately encouraging up to fifty people, from babies to grandmas, from churchwardens to those on the outer fringe of the church, those with many skills and those who needed looking after. These included people who had never travelled out of Leeds or dared to arrange a holiday for themselves before. It was marvellous when people eventually opted out of the annual parish holiday, having found the confidence and motivation to go away as a family on their own. For five days we would rent a self-catering hostel in a remote area, perhaps near the sea or the mountains, or ideally both. Through those days of relaxing, walking, caving, abseiling, canoeing, sight-seeing, eating, drinking, cooking, washing up and cleaning together, everyone had the chance of deepening their sense of belonging to the community and testing out their capacity for aspiring to the Christian virtue of love and forgiveness.

It could be an opportunity almost unconsciously to test out with others your experiences of marriage, child-rearing and sharing family life. I remember a widow, Annie, who had had a hard life and has since died, who came on one holiday in the Lake District. One morning I met her standing in rapt attention looking up the staircase of the farmhouse in which we were staying. "What are you looking at, Annie?" I asked. "Father," she said, indicating a young man sweeping down the stairs, "in forty years of marriage I never found out a man could handle a sweeping brush."

Such an experience is also an opportunity for preparing a very free style of eucharistic celebration, with many people participating in a way which would be unlikely in a formal church setting. This created a very definite lever for change back in the parish. Patterns of authority, leadership and spirituality arise up from those who are in other circumstances not confident to offer a great deal. A sense of mutual care and deep friendship among all age groups is fostered, which leaves a permanent mark on the individual and the parish itself.

I also found that an ambitious drama production, locally written, involving four months of gestation, drawing together a total team of actors, carpenters, musicians, costume makers and so on, of perhaps a hundred, across the age boundaries, produces similar results. Many parishes do this I know, and on their own such events seem unremarkable, but in the pursuit of a little light relief as well as a way of learning to be a reconciling community, as back-up to a strenuous community programme of mission, such events have a powerfully transforming capacity to build up the Body of Christ in a style that can communicate with local people.

Looking back on this now, I have to ask myself how far I acted consistently. On the one hand I have been speaking passionately about the importance of allowing people to "be the Church" without changing their culture, and on the other, of introducing people to experiences of drama and hill-walking which could be seen as me imposing my preferences and skills on them. I think the esential point I'm trying to make is that while church life may well broaden members' world-view in countless challenging ways, it must never do so at the expense of accepting and respecting local people just as they are. The Kingdom of God is at work long before our church or our vicar begin to make their mark, and we should say or do nothing that contradicts that truth. You don't have to be a Yuppy to be a Christian.

Earlier we saw how the New Testament teaches that the Spirit gives to each one differing gifts to fulfil various ministries. The parish president needs to trust and be accepted in his charism of discernment. He must pray constantly that the Spirit will preserve him from appointing anyone to a task which is too difficult or for which he or she has no aptitude. But there is the insidious danger that the tests we use will be all too human: does he or she speak with received pronunciation? Are they on the telephone? Do they know how to write minutes? In other words, are we merely re-emphasizing the world's view of power and importance? If instead we can risk a variety of styles within one community then we shall begin to discover that the Church is able to be the vehicle of the Gospel of Christ for a much wider spectrum of people of all ages: where the teacher, the fire officer, the psychiatric out-patient, the theatre box-office worker, the hospital administrator, the road gritter, the unemployed, the keepers of the post office and the clerk in the textile trade can share a common life in Christ. Constantly we need to reflect on Jesus' words, "It shall not be so among you". Working people will not come to church today out of a sense of duty or tradition or to be lorded over and patronized. But if we turn upside down the world's standards, in the Church, everyone can learn to see more value in themselves as in God's sight, and to trust their own styles of doing things, and this puts the onus on the wider Church to begin quickly to affirm and encourage such a move. That is where a really local ministry can begin, drawing in and bringing out the humanity of so many people, who are not important in the world's eyes.

Church leadership does not need to be so formal, so remote or so solemn as we have often practised it in the recent past. There are many styles of working-class leadership which we hardly notice, never mind engage in the Church's work. How often in working-class parishes it is only on the few who drive in from the neighbouring suburban parish that the mantle of responsibility and honour falls. Can we aim to multiply examples of leadership of a kind which responds to situations as they arise? Suppose, for example, a lorry runs into the front of someone's house in the inner city. The people who would rush out and deal with the situation and board up the house would not be the usual leaders but the people with manual skills who are used to devising ingenious ways of dealing with fresh situations. There would not be a dominant leader in the team that would form to do the job, but everyone would contribute their own ideas and skills. Once the job was done, they would take up their existing relationship again without any one person having taken on a peculiar permanent role or status. However, it has to be honestly admitted that to get the balance right between the one appointed to preside and yet the one who wishes to be regarded as part of a leadership team, is very difficult. Not to get depressed or unnerved while trying to be president rather than dictator, faced with some parishioners who have a long tradition of regarding shared decision-taking as weakness and who yearn for a remote and confident aristocratic figure on whom they can be totally dependent, requires dedication to one's own spiritual pilgrimage and a clearly articulated theology of the Church.

As is increasingly to be found in many parishes, those who were prepared to share with me in taking seriously their ministry in the parish found it helpful to have a few simple structures to enable a new vision of the Church to begin to come to life. To this end our church community was for several years administered jointly by four groups, all with lay chairmen and composed partly of members of the Church Council and partly of others in the congregation. Each member of the Council was expected to serve on one of the groups. These four committees were set up to deal with all main decisions under the headings of Mission, Development, Fabric and Social. We opted for four groups as an alternative to a proliferation of too many groups, which our congregation could never have sustained.

The Social group had an obvious function, and despite lack of confidence was eventually encouraged to take initiatives rather than merely to respond to requests from me. All too often parish social life consists of thinking up activities (or worse still, repeating last year's) to entertain people or to finance the church from the blackmailed giving of non-members. There is all the difference in the world when the social life is seen as cementing and testing out the community's ability to be true to its ideals: actually to become a community that not only worships together but is a body of loving, reconciling friends. In this way the social life of the parish can almost become an acting out of the liturgical exchange of the Peace. It is a commitment to become brother and sister to others, a recognition that, although there will be differences of opinion, peace is always on the agenda. By learning to become companions with one another, God's people, who are given to us warts an' all rather than chosen or selected by us, we can hope to become companions with the whole of society, especially when our preference might be quite different.

The Fabric group under its lay Buildings Administrator really did take full responsibility for the administration and maintenance of church property. A practical man in the early stages of retirement can take all the worry of buildings off the shoulders of a priest, if we can let go radically and not keep interfering and changing the rules. Also, if this administrator can share with a team of practical people the detailed planning of repairs and major projects, money can be saved, ideas be genuinely shared throughout the congregation and real corporate responsibility be discovered.

The Mission group dealt with mission in its broadest sense; they supported overseas mission and mission in the parish; they were also responsible for building up a team to work with the clergy in visiting, for local ecumenical contacts and for producing the parish magazine. All this is quite commonplace in middle-class parishes today, but much more precarious in a less confident urban setting.

Regarding the question of visiting, although we frequently hear of teams of laity and clergy together tackling all kinds of pastoral situations, including the administration of Holy Communion to the housebound, the memory of those great priests who single-handed spent so much time visiting earlier in the century, will take a long time to be erased from the memories and expectations of older parishioners. To make the transition from a solo ministry of visiting to team work on the part of the clergy requires a strong assurance that this is the right response to a completely changed environment. I should like to pay tribute here to those who served with me in Halton as assistant priests, of whom I say more in a separate chapter. Whilst I concentrated on trying to work out the right model of presidency, they so often protected the sick and housebound from neglect by their own important ministries. The process of reformation is bound to leave some painful corners, and it is true that, even with a new vision of parish life, the clergy can only hand over what the laity have been prepared to receive. I was grateful to the assistant priests who often shielded the laity from my single-mindedness!

The Development group, in close collaboration with the Fabric group and continually nurtured by the clergy, had its most difficult challenge in re-ordering the church building for modern liturgy. Soon after my arrival in the parish the Church Council revealed its keenness to set up a working party to investigate the possibility of changing to the Series 3 eucharist (the immediate precursor of Rite A in the *Alternative Service Book* 1980). In the parish magazine, in groups and at parish meetings we offered everyone the chance to begin to discover the church as a communion. This process helped most people to realize that the words of the new services would be muted in power if they were restricted by traditional but no longer appropriate actions, gestures and furnishings. A great deal of stress entered the community's life as those who were excited enough about the new possibilities tried to persuade the others, who had perhaps not been to parish meetings and who placed more weight on the continuity of the church's appearance than on its role of continually adapting to allow its people's life and commitment to be fully articulated.

We had several skirmishes over moving curtains, screens and altar rails, and about spending money on a new altar, sanctuary space, furniture, carpet and lighting. There seemed to be a clear parallel between the gradual change in understanding of the people's role in the church and their changes in attitude to the building. On the one hand some began with the image of a formal, changeless, "normal" group of "nice" people, and moved to one of a sharing, outgoing community, constantly on pilgrimage; in a similar way some who began with the "heritage" or shrine attitude towards the building, almost believing that God or the Christian faith was incarcerated in the bricks and mortar and the way things always had been, moved to a more functional view of the building, seeing it as a theatre or room for worship to be used and adjusted in whatever way would best assist the worshippers to experience God's presence in communion with others. I remember stressing, when announcing far-reaching changes to the layout of the church, that each and every member of the Council was equally responsible by mentioning them all by name.

Despite all the theories of shared responsibility, the hairs on the back of my neck stood up on the day when you couldn't see across the church for brick-dust and couldn't hear yourself speak for the sound of pneumatic drills. How was I to have known that the 1930s builders supported even light wooden screens with two-foot-long steel posts set in con-crete? Though patience has its rewards. One member of the Church Council originally very anxious about the proposed alterations and who had abstained in the voting, was overheard six months later showing off the church proudly to Australian visitors with the remark: "Just see what we've done, it's made such a difference to our worship." The Development group was also responsible for the spiritual nurture of the congregation; they arranged house groups, quiet days, parish weekends and preparation for baptism.

This is not to say that I see no place for clerical authority or leadership. Far from it. It is a matter of rediscovering in this context what role the Church is giving to the priest, and this is itself a quest with its own agenda that will last for decades to come. I have an unshakeable conviction that it is possible, while encouraging decision-making by the laity, to exercise a priestly authority which is primarily a spiritual one rather than merely practical or concentrated on details of admin-istration, though in practice it is inevitable that a parish priest will sometimes feel convinced of the need to exert pressure, subtle or otherwise, to lead the parish in a particular direction. There were particular issues in my time when it seemed right to "drive" a decision. For example, about having regular services and parish activities on the council estate to make it clear that it was as much part of the parish as anywhere else and should be treated as such, or again regarding giving away generously at the end of the Church's year even if that meant starting the new financial year with just a few pounds in the bank, or again to make sure we confidently re-ordered our building to express in the euch-arist what we were growing to feel about our common life. No doubt in an ideal church this would never be necessary, and it is a responsibility a priest will surely wish to exercise cautiously and sparingly, rather than as the norm, and even then only in the context of teaching and full discussion. We don't have an ideal church and we can't wait for ever to reach a consensus about some vital points that affect the church's identity as an apostolic community. St Paul didn't have ideal churches to work with either, so that along with the gifts of service, there was needed in the Pauline churches a hierarchy of sorts, if only to combat enthusiasm. Schillebeeckx in his writing admits that this was so and a necessary and proper aspect of Paul's ministry and of the representative, presi-dential, ministerial priesthood today. It is an essential part of my own vision that priests have a very real responsibility to share in the government of the Church, though some misunderstand shared ministry to evacuate the clergy's role and allow no place for the priest to speak as representative, chief pastor and as one sharing the bishop's *episcopé* (oversight). Just occasionally laity should heed the words of Edith Sitwell, "I don't teach plumbers how to plumb", and accept that the training and experience of the clergy equip them in a unique way. Though after centuries of emphasis on such a style, it will naturally take a while to get the proper balance. What will be under scrutiny at the point where the priest presses a definite course of action will be his motiva-tion, his honest awareness of the common mind of the parish, as well as his adherence to his own spiritual pilgrimage.

We had other problems that the Church Council had to face. In particular, how far should the Council and the clergy trust a committee to take initiatives and see their plans through without them having to be rehearsed in detail at the full meetings? From the beginning we asked the chairmen of the working groups to submit agendas and minutes to clergy, wardens, and the parish secretary, to make sure we all had an opportunity to know what was happening and to attend meetings if that seemed appropriate. We also found that if the Church Council secretary made a short synopsis of the principal decisions of the groups that had met between Council meetings, it could be circulated to everyone concerned. On the Council agenda we regularly had an item when questions arising from these synopses could be put to the relevant chairmen, so saving the automatic rehearsal of all that the groups were doing. Especially when the groups were really working hard, for example in the autumn, planning for Christmas and Eastertime, far more thought and imaginative schemes could be introduced into parish life than if it had been left just to the clergy.

I know some parish clergy who at Council meetings normally invite the deputy chairman, usually one of the wardens, to act as chairman. Their reasons for doing this are to give the deputy a real sense of responsibility, and to allow the priest the freedom to take part in debates without the constraint of being the chairman and to express the clergy's desire to be seen primarily as one of the congregation. I tried this myself for a short while but found it more confusing than helpful. Really I think it is quite possible to act as chairman and still make your points without preventing others from speaking. However, I am ever cautious of the style of the Rector under whom I served as a curate, who used to spend hours preparing first rate speeches, presenting his arguments like a barrister. Of course he usually got what he was after because no one else, tired after a busy day at work, had the mental energy or the knowledge to counter his careful arguments. I am aware too that Canon Tiller in his Report, *A Strategy for the Church's Ministry* (1983), perceives that a president is required for the liturgy, a chairman for the decision-making process, and the oversight of the congregation needs a pastor who may well work in a team with others, and the three tasks need not necessarily be filled by the same person. Returning to the Church Council at Halton, I came to see that as far as we were concerned the one who presided over the whole life of the community, who was the natural one to preside at the eucharist (in collaboration with other clergy on the team), had the responsibility to preside over the meeting. There was no reason, however, why he should misuse his position to prevent fair debate, to manipulate or be heavy-handed.

The basic administration I have just described served us well for five years, allowing many members of the congregation to learn to feel responsible. Looking back now I see that they did remarkably well, in that at first I failed to see how basic a grasp of the essentials and practice of the faith even key parishioners can have, and I also failed to recognize the importance of training people in the simple techniques of leadership so as to be able to lead others on to greater participation. Basic shyness so often holds lay people back from making the same demands on others that they make upon themselves. I can think of a conscientious and over-worked woman who would rather spend five hours ill-advisedly counting the contents of charity collection envelopes herself than "spoil Sunday afternoon" for several other people.

Above all we needed the Spirit to come among us in a more powerful way. We needed to turn prayers in a book into real prayers. We needed the power of the Spirit to help us to heal, to forgive, to inspire and to bring confidence and joy. It occurred to a number of us about the same time that the congregation would benefit greatly from having a mission specifically to itself. The preparations we had to make for eighteen months towards a Franciscan Discovery Fortnight, under the flamboyant guidance of Brother Peter Douglas SSF, proved to be a time for a great deal of learning and growth for myself and others. We saw that, without the Spirit, even the most wonderful structures are just not enough; we realized how hungry many were for a real knowledge of Christ in the sacraments, the scriptures and private prayer. We realized how poor was our evangelistic energy and direction, and how difficult other people found it to establish themselves among us. A great deal of personal growth took place during the eighteen months before the Discovery Fortnight: leaders for house groups were trained; we had a procession of witness; we planned a new, more direct style of parish magazine; a pastoral team for visiting really got off the ground; we made some plans for teaching the faith to the families who asked for infant baptism; we developed a freer style of music in worship and compiled our own hymns and songs book.

All this happened as a direct response to the call to prepare for the Discovery Fortnight "One with Us". Even if the arrival of the friars had suddenly been cancelled, a great deal would have already taken place. The Franciscan Team arrived, and having complimented us on our thorough preparations, deliberately turned everything upside down and took away all the security we had in rotas and systems. It was as if we had painstakingly built up a great bonfire and they came along and set fire to it. During the Mission, with its house groups, events, parties, prayer and moving worship, there were moments when we wondered whether the whole thing would be just quickly reduced to ashes or whether we should be cooking on it for a long time to come. In the end the latter is clearly the case. A great spirit of new love for Christ and commitment to serving him in the world through the

Church rose up among us. Individuals who had been searching for a long time came to new levels of perception and pledged themselves to work it out in practice at home, at work, in the church and the wider community. It was important for the clergy to be free to receive the mission, and it was an unusual time because we had no worship to plan and were deliberately excluded from the house groups so that they would not be inhibited by our presence.

There are members of the congregation who actually found the mission more threatening than helpful. This was largely a reaction against the Franciscan concentration on prayer, informality and happiness, and their obvious lack of enthusiasm for rotas, forward planning and recognition of social or ecclesiastical status, clerical or lay. But many were helped, not least by the very combination of moving liturgy and quiet informal times of prayer, of emotionally charged healing services and occasions of total silence, of generosity with time and energy for those in need and a sharp challenge to the indisciplined, the lazy or community trouble-makers. There were tears of joy and penitence, anger and hilarity. In one fortnight many emotional triggers were loosed in homes, in worship, in study of the faith and in personal relationships in the congregation. From an unlooked-for incident when one of the Franciscan brothers, having visited an ex-prisoner holding down a job in Birmingham, was mugged late one Saturday evening in Leeds bus station, came a great outpouring of grace on the whole congregation. The friar concerned testified in church the next morning to his forgiveness of the six unknown youths who had beaten him up, saying, "I can only feel sorry for them that they have nothing else in their lives so that they think that's a good thing to do on a Saturday night". He was in great pain and could hardly open his mouth, though he did not know at the time he had a fractured cheekbone and that his sight and memory would be permanently impaired. New vocations of several kinds have become clear, and no doubt there will be others to follow.

It would be impossible and undesirable that all parishes should have a jolting and encouraging visit from the Franciscans in all their various moods, prompting thoughts like "No one expects the Spanish Inquisition". I remember that when Brother Peter Douglas first descended on us after we had put in a request for a mission, to "check us out", he was very clear in his demands upon the Church Council, spelling out that there were nine other parishes he and his team could easily go to help if we didn't seem keen enough. Once in every ten years or so, I am sure that every parish that's doing its best should have the stimulation and encouragement of that kind of experience provided by whatever outside group seems most appropriate, although in the meantime there is every reason for exploring the D.I.Y. method of Parish Audit stimulated by the *Faith in the City* report.

Afterwards it was a perilous business to keep a balance between allowing the Spirit to go on working over a long period without the restriction of "normal" parish life, and the danger of assuming that new ideas and intentions generated in the Discovery Fortnight would immediately find a cutting edge in parish life without help and encouragement. We decided that the Church Council on its own could not follow up all that had to be done, and the previous structures seemed inadequate, so a temporary plan was drawn up. In this the Council held two groups responsible for detailed every-day practicalities – Fabric maintenance and Music and Worship, including planning ahead, hymn choosing, choir, a more informal music group, servers, sacristy and so on. The new initiatives we placed for the time being in the care of the chief officers of the parish plus a few others, with the umbrella title, "Sharing the Faith Project".

At a parish meeting held just after our Discovery Fortnight, under the chairmanship of our suffragan bishop, we asked the diocese for permission to allow baptized but unconfirmed children in the congregation to share fully in the eucharist. We recognized that this might cause some discomfort for the children when they worshipped outside the parish, or when they had to explain their position to other clergy, but that the insight we had gained was worth pursuing. Our communion policy was to admit children of parents who so desired at about the age of eight, after a short course in which the children did some basic learning about what the eucharist means. Essentially we felt we had gained a renewed understanding of the whole congregation, of whatever age, as the People of God, each called to discover and live out our vocation bestowed by baptism. From this self-understanding there grew an uneasiness with the exclusion of children from a central part of the Church's life. We were encouraged in this approach by the Church of England's Report, chaired by Bishop John Dennis, *Communion before Confirmation?* (1985) and the World Council of Churches Faith and Order Paper No. 109, *. . . and do not hinder them*. The latter reinforces my own view that whatever we do about children in church, unless they enjoy it and feel they belong now as much as anyone else, we are not doing justice to our understanding of the nature of the work of the Holy Spirit in baptism or of the psychological needs of the children themselves. Whatever we say to children about our faith and about the importance of prayer, it is what we *do* and what they themselves pick up with us, that has any profound effect. As one mother is quoted in the Faith and Order Paper:

It does not worry me that when our children, aged, say, two and a half, first started receiving bread and wine they thought of it as picnic bread and participated largely because they were imitating me. Their sense of belonging to the group and of being like everyone else was an important part of their development. It was important that we deliberately expected them to sing hymns and to say "Amen" at the end of prayers, even though they did not understand all the words. We wanted the children to know that they came to join in as much as they could and as they were. Gradually the words of the institution began to have meaning, and the bread and wine were related to them and to the world; they would not have done so in the same way had they not felt they belonged.

Quoted by John M. Sutcliffe in
*Children and Holy Communion*,
WCC Faith and Order Paper No. 109, 1982.

Small action groups with some of the atmosphere of basic Christian Communities were then set up under this Project for the training of a team to engage in baptism preparation for families, the instruction of children who were to receive Holy Communion on the strength of their baptism rather than confirmation, the new magazine as an agent of mission, the Pastoral Team and ecumenical developments. We also came to a new realization of the potential of social events (as such rather than for fund-raising) for helping fringe church members to become more confident. So we remained committed to the notion that a parish that truly shares in ministry (rather than merely the laity "helping" the clergy) will need constantly evolving structures, which never become too important or immutable, which together with regular parish meetings are the only way of making sure that as many people as wish have a role in being the local church as appropriate to their gifts. To avoid confusion I do want to stress again here that I am not suggesting that those who give their all to a demanding home, job or caring agency like the Samaritans should be expected to have a time-consuming ministry in the parish as well. Probably we all have to adjust to varying responsibilities at different stages of life, and it is important never to assume that the elderly retired or the young enquirers are to become passive receivers of ministry rather than bringing their wisdom and gifts in appropriate ways.

# 7

# Supporting the Strong

The priest has the responsibility of offering careful support to the people he has motivated to ministry, as they seek to fulfil their vocations. Most clergy and members of religious orders take some kind of spiritual direction or confession for granted. Theological colleges have often encouraged students to adopt an experienced priest to whom they could resort with their dusty soul once or more often each year. Especially where this has proved to be a rewarding exercise, the habit will have stuck. The logic is unquestionable, that those who are on the front line in ministry should themselves be ministered to. In recent years small groups of clergy (often described as "cells"), sometimes with their wives as well, have met together, several times a year, to support one another and share their burdens in confidence. Some theological colleges and dioceses have created structures to encourage clergy to consider the voluntary appraisal of their ministry by another priest, of either their own choice or drawn from a small panel of priests and lay people trained for the task. The point of the exercise, for the ordained ministers' sakes and for the sake of the Church they serve, is to be offered an opportunity to be helped to assess their strengths and weaknesses, their use of time, and their particular needs for in-service training. Until now only a tiny minority of lay people, often either those with close associations with a religious community or those in the regular habit of going on retreat, have had the benefit of regular spiritual direction and the sacrament of reconciliation. But amongst the laity this has been regarded until quite recently as eccentric, almost the harmless self-indulgence of those who make religion a hobby. Yet as a parish priest I came to believe that it is vital, for everyone concerned, especially for those who are increasingly recognizing that there should be a unity between their practice of the faith and the fulfilment of their daily obligations, and therefore the understanding of their role in the parish, at home, and at work as Christian ministry.

It is possible to isolate a number of trends which are changing the climate of spiritual guidance amongst the laity. In the field of literature, Kenneth Leech's *Soul Friend*, published almost ten years ago, reminded the Church of the vital role played by spiritual guides throughout the Christian centuries, and powerfully advocated the reintroduction of this ministry as a quite ordinary, rather than élitist, element of church life. Leech's inspiration encouraged me to offer, within my own limited capabilities, the opportunity for a good number of lay people to find help in their struggle to be faithful disciples.

A second trend is the involvement of increasing numbers of lay people in challenging renewal movements outside parish structures. Individuals within such popular movements, which are focuses of growth in faithful disciple-ship, no longer confined to those describing themselves as "catholic", are developing rules of life or beginning to turn to the idea of spiritual guidance.

A third strand in this diagnosis is that our perception of who is ministering on the front line is gradually changing. In the past we placed too much value on hard-pressed clergy, with their single-minded dedication, even at the risk of health and family, working with the model of being eaten alive by those whom they were dedicated to serve. Where this pattern is changing and laity are being released and empowered for ministries within the Church – visiting the sick, the bereaved, the parents of those to be baptized, planning the liturgy or some piece of social action; where parish life is becoming less activity-orientated and taking on the vision of a whole community collaborating in mission, through a variety of channels there is an urgent need for ministry to the ministers.

It is quite irresponsible to allow lay people to offer ministry to others unless they are seriously struggling with their own inner journey. Nor, as most clergy recognize for themselves, should anyone presume to be active on the ministerial front line without the support of a spiritual guide. In the present climate of ministry, more than ever the church needs to be confident about becoming a power house of spiritual sustenance. There is an insidious paternalism if the clergy continue to maintain the mysti que that the following of the clerical way is so superior in quality that it requires guidance automatically, but it is a matter of choice for the committed lay person.

And fourthly, in the wake of so much new emphasis on parish-based ministries for lay people, we have been helped by *Faith in the City* and the preparations for the Roman Catholic Synod on the laity in 1987, to recall that for the majority of people their ministry will always lie in the office, on the motorway, on the wholesale market, in the home, school, in Parliament, in the hospital, laboratory, on the stock exchange. There is an urgent need to offer one-to-one guidance to Christians engaged in every area of service to humanity, as this quotation from one of the preparation groups for the Roman Catholic 1987 Synod on the laity makes plain:

> How does one live a Christian vocation in the cabinet of a modern state or in a multinational corporation and the World Bank? What sort of Christian Witness can be given by Trade Union

leaders? What can lay people do about global unemployment or racialism? In my view there needs to be a serious . . . [reflection] on the real issues facing lay people in the church and their every-day experiences in the parish and basic Christian community or organization, and in their every-day lives at home in a family life, in changing community life, at work with employment changes associated with structural transformations, in their membership of minority or immigrant groups, their sense of powerlessness and alienation and so on.

Peter Verity, "The Christian-in-the-World",
*Priests and People*, Vol. 1, No. 2.

How are we to set about this? In the past we have left this business to a few specialists who were clearly recognized to be filled with the Spirit. There is no doubt that direction calls for holiness and repentance in the one who offers it, but I perceive a rapidly expanding need for this work and, therefore, many who would not immediately consider themselves typecast as spiritual directors will need in humility to offer their services. In my own experience as a parish priest, faced with people in need of such help, together with the clear challenge offered by Kenneth Leech's writings, I decided to make an attempt at spiritual guidance. I well remember the scepticism of an elderly and wise priest who thought I meant to inflict a watered-down clerical spirituality on to the laity. Conscious of my own limitations, it did occur to me when I started that it could actually be a decided advantage to be closer to the spiritual state of those one was trying to help, rather than to be so far advanced in the life of prayer that the laity would despair of my even understanding them. For this reason the ordinary parish priest, if he can be honest about his own struggles with his often sketchy prayer life, may be just the right person to help the laity in their needs, even having to suffer the pain of them eventually reaching beyond his own limits. This is not at all the same as off-loading clerical spirituality on to lay people.

One of the most important tasks of spiritual direction, surely, recognizing the dangers in our day of the proliferation of so many partial and inadequate representations of the Christian life, is to help Christians to a full maturity, which includes the receiving and celebrating of God's Word and sacrament in community, trying to be incarnated into the world, to serve our brothers and sisters in their needs and to work for social justice. The primary concern is not with high-powered talk about spiritual paths, which can be in itself a protection from allowing God to get to us, but rather to concentrate on the qualities of discipleship required in each one trying to work through their vocation as a member of the Body of Christ. If each baptized person is called to the fullness of Christian life, he or she desperately needs to know they are not alone, that there is no need to despair about their life of prayer, that there is a shoulder to cry on, and someone to bring Christ's reassurance of forgiveness and grace.

One of the dominant moods of the new way of being Church that is evolving is the positive expectation that everyone has a contribution to make. Parish priests can, I believe, take people by storm, gently but winningly, explaining in their own words something of the notion of spiritual direction, and inviting them to enter into that which Leech summarizes as:

> a relationship of friendship in Christ between two people by which one is enabled, through the personal encounter, to discern more clearly the will of God for one's life, and to grow in discipleship and in the life of grace.

The first meeting is surely the hardest for both parties. However, if it is made clear that it is not a lecture, nor a judgemental session, nor an attempt to make one dependent upon the other, but genuinely a chance to speak and to be listened to in total confidence, in a place where there is little chance of disturbance, it will usually be greeted with relief. Here at last is the opportunity to ask questions about prayer, about difficulties at home or at work, to talk about anything at all, to admit ignorance or anger about particular matters in private, to have your vicar's total undivided attention for an hour. This is not the same as a good gossip about the world in general and some people in particular. The mental agenda I would always have would cover worship, prayer, study, the pursuit of ministry, life styles and giving, but basically we have to try to be aware of the individual's need to spend time on whatever is their major concern at that moment. Another significant area of discussion can often be helping the individual to grasp at his or her level an understanding of modern liturgical practice or the subleties of the current theological tensions, in a way quite different from what is possible from the pulpit.

When approached with a serious and confidential but nevertheless light touch, I have found its value to be immense. In busy churches today, clergy and lay people often end up talking hurriedly about crises or the practical matters surrounding buildings, music or pastoral ministries. The task of presiding over a Christian community inevitably demands of the presiding priest skills of management and discernment, and yet a central element in this is the pastoral care of those among whom he has evoked ministerial skills. Active lay people can quickly become exhausted if they are simply drained without being nourished. I know how many potential crises were nipped in the bud through this approach. How easy it is for the clergy to assume that all is well unless we actually allow people to speak their minds, and really listen, even when what we hear might not always be to our liking. However, we have to be on our guard that such a relationship does not degenerate into one of control, where the clergy begin to exercise a more subtle proprietorship than the one we are trying to grow out of.

I regard this approach to ministry as an essential response to need, though clergy will vary in their capacity both to offer such a relationship to a growing number of people and consciously to shed other loads in order to have the reserves to do it well. For this reason, together with the clear tradition in the past, we should encourage Spirit-filled lay people to offer this ministry to other laity. Some clergy (though not religious) might be shocked at this, perhaps considering the damage that irresponsible guidance could cause. The grace of ordination is no guarantee that a clergyman will be better fitted to offer spiritual guidance than a lay person, and if we are realistic we must recognize that this already happens in a number of ways. Informally, lay people have always helped one another through difficult patches of their lives. Where the catechetical method of preparing people for the sacraments is employed, members of a lay teaching team act as spiritual guides to the candidates, and there is no reason why this should not continue indefinitely; also, within the Third Order of St Francis, for example, lay people are sometimes appointed to act as a guide for another; the members of religious orders used by some as guides, are often lay people; and I know of examples where two lay people agree mutually to be soul friend to one another, neither being clear exactly who is helping whom.

Some people might be happy to have a lay person involved in direction if they were trained and commissioned by the Church. My immediate response is that official recognition by the bishop, plus a piece of paper, is far less telling than the genuine authorization of being one known to be travelling the road of baptismal discipleship sufficiently clearly to be able to help others. Authority from the congregation is more valuable than authorization by the diocese, both because a proliferation of commissioned lay ministries is bound to leave some people exercising ministry without official recognition, feeling second-class as well as undermining the basic premise that baptism is everyone's commission to ministry. Once when I discussed the question of training for this ministry with an older priest he reacted negatively, implying that some have the gift and some don't. "They'll be wanting training for prophets next!" He was even suspicious of people who write about such matters. There is something attractive about this laissez-faire attitude that everyone recognizes and uses a good confessor or director, rather like the trusted retreat conductor. However, if we are to mobilize far more priests and laity for this work, and regard it as a high priority for a parish committed to collaborative ministry, is it not possible to consider some enhancing of natural but latent skills?

Discussion of the skills of spiritual direction is in its infancy in the Church of England, with exceptions such as the writings of Martin Thornton and Kenneth Leech. Gordon Jeff's important work through SPIDIR, of running courses for spiritual directors, operates at a low-profile level, though it is gradually becoming recognized among Anglicans that some training is possible and right. On the other hand, Roman Catholic periodicals frequently carry advertisements for extended courses of training in spiritual direction. Some find it helpful to be taught some basic skills in counselling and spiritual direction, with an introduction to inner healing. The Redemptorists regularly run an intensive course, lasting two weeks, in which participants learn to enhance their basic talents by working on their own every-day problems in small groups, under supervision and in the context of a balanced diet of prayer, worship, rest, study, silence and companionship. There is a real sense in which one begins from within one's own brokenness and constant need of renewal. No one should enter into such a course with a view to becoming anything so crude as an expert in direction, but what does it say if a would-be director is not prepared to stand under an experienced person to engage in some challenging praying and thinking? My own reflection on this experience, after eight years of attempting spiritual direction in a parish, was that I realized how poor our average standard of listening can be. Richard Holloway has recently pointed out that the key for Christian counselling is the discipline of listening, the ability to empty ourselves of ourselves, at least to some extent, so that others may fill us. So often we are only half-listening, poised ready to speak as soon as the other leaves off, or too quick to give good advice. On the course in which I took part, we learned gradually how the greater part of our human inter-communication is beyond words, and to what a great extent our society plays down the importance of feelings in favour of thinking and speaking.

No one should claim too much for such training but it brought together laity, clergy, and religious, all of whom in their own contexts are attempting the important task of direction and solving conflicts between members of the communities of which they are charged with the oversight. There was not only the input of the teaching, geared at a very practical level, but a renewal of Christian love and reconciliation in the small groups. The training reinforced the need for directors to allow themselves the dignity to allow time for reading, proper rest, and solitude. No one really wants a spiritual director who is tired and inattentive and gives no time to study. In the common life of this training course we lived out the tensions between the development of the corporate life of the Church, called to salvation as a community, and the individual relationship to God, which are at the heart of so many modern divisions in the Church.

We lived together as a searching community, learning to listen and observe which part of the Church's resources of prayer, teaching, or ministry were most appropriate for each other at different times. This was a very adequate model for the role of the spiritual directors of the Church today. He or she can best help people by the deliberate cultivation of the crucial art of slow, sensitive listening to what is actually being said, combined with a constantly developing and lived awareness of the riches of the Christian inheritance, and an ability to discern how to put the one in touch with the other.

In particular I cherish the reminder that no one should criticize another until they have walked two miles in their shoes, and also that no one really knows what the other person wants to be understood about them until they have spoken their last word.

The important work of listening, guiding and healing cannot be left just to the clergy, but inevitably it depends on their vision if this vital ministry of support is to become widely available to those offering leadership in church communities. Sadly, all too often the clergy seem to be moving too quickly. Laity say that their vicar is too busy or too over-worked for them to dream of asking him to sit down for an hour and listen to them. The same clergy so often respond aggressively to the suggestion that we should adopt a strategy and work out more precisely what our role should be, as all too much geared towards "management" at the expense of "priesthood". This is an important challenge to everyone in ordained ministry, to re-examine what it is we are so busy doing. Are we not so often taking away other people's rightful ministry, by doing it ourselves, and yet at the same time, being so fully occupied, we have no energy to assist others in their development. If we genuinely wish to rediscover the integral place of lay people in the life and mission of the Church, one immensely significant and highly appropriate way, well attested in the Church's tradition, is the encouragement of many, who are currently making strong attempts to be ministers of many kinds, to enter into a voluntary relationship with a spiritual director.

# 8

# The Parish Communion

Interviewed on the video, *Beneath the Surface*, John Yates, the Bishop of Gloucester, replies "No" to the perennial question, "Do I have to go to church to be a Christian?" But immediately he qualifies this as being only a half-truth, because to call yourself a Christian and never or very rarely to go to church is to live on the spiritual capital of someone else. The Bishop is right, but for anyone visiting many different churches on Sunday, it's not difficult to see why only a small percentage of the population attend these days.

As we examine our parish life, urgently we must ask, is it focused on the worship of God in Trinity? For most Church of England parishes today, and despite the growth of monthly family services, the central act of worship on Sunday is the Parish Communion. It would be easy enough, and many writers have done it at length, to be very critical of much of our church's worship. I will confine myself to saying that it is often unattractive, boring, clerically-dominated, ill-prepared, with few signs in the preaching, choice of hymns or ordering of the building that reveal either awe in God's presence or a commitment to working with him in the wider world. At the heart of a committed missionary Christian community, there needs to be profound, stirring and lively worship.

One parish I know say very clearly, in defence of their traditional Book of Common Prayer, that they find it totally satisfies their needs. They admit disappointment that no young people feel moved to go to church, but insist that unless or until they do, no change is necessary in the form or style of their services.

On the whole question of church membership, I can recognize the human motivations that bring some in and keep most out. A traditional way of life for some people of all ages includes church attendance; some lonely and broken people will always find consolation in church membership; some men in particular are fulfilled through the limited responsibilities and authority that come with being, for example, a church treasurer, though the need for frequent attendance is not always perceived as coinciding with the holding of such responsibilities. Individual patterns of worship vary considerably. One lady I met recently told me she was sorry that she wouldn't be hearing me preach at the patronal festival, because that would be in the morning and she only ever attended evensong and a monthly eight o'clock communion service. Another faithful Church Council member assured me that his regular devotion was mowing the church grass.

Now that I am no longer the vicar of an urban congregation, whose future is always precarious by contrast with the confident and often full-to-capacity suburban church, it is easy to be wise and liberal about church membership. In the parish, I taught that anyone who was seriously hoping to grow in Christ needed the regular strength of the sacrament of Holy Communion and of being in fellowship with the others. I believe we avoided some of the worst dangers of sectarianism, but for theological and practical reasons it seemed right to have a high expectation of people's commitment to the Christian pilgrimage to be measured in this way. Just as in terms of ministry, for most people I presented a high positive expectation, so turning a dependent people into a ministering body, this has implications for the regular and frequent celebration of the Holy

Communion. In parish life we were moving away from the supermarket or pub mentality. The analogy of the pub can be a helpful one in describing negatively the way of being Church which is very prevalent in society but which offers no realistic future for the heart of Christianity. You may patronize a particular local pub because your father went there before you, you like the architecture or nostalgic atmosphere, or because you like the landlord, or his wife or the way the beer is kept. But you feel no commitment, because the pub belongs to a remote brewery. Isn't this how many, if not most, people view their parish church? I remember people frequently ringing me "to book the church" for a wedding, and how I was sorely tempted to ask if they'd like me to be there as well.

In ministry and worship, my aim was to transform a group of people who happened to "go to church" into a true community of the baptized, in which each saw their hope of salvation and their proper share in Christ's ministry within the People of God.

The Parish and People Movement of the 1950s achieved a great deal in re-establishing the eucharist, in the form of the Parish Communion, at the heart of the Church of England's life. Imaginatively approached, the parish mass atmosphere can vary tremendously from week to week, offering as appropriate to the worshippers the various aspects of Christ's saving presence, gathering up the strands of the community's developing life, helping the assembled individuals to become a ministering and missionary body.

The publication in 1980 of the *Alternative Service Book* provided just the trigger mechanism which we needed in Halton to allow the regular 9.30 a.m. service to become the vehicle of the weekly nourishment of a collaborative congregation. In describing here some of the practical steps we took, I want to record how much I recognize we inherited from previous years of worshipping and teaching. To say that some things seemed more appropriate in the eighties is not necessarily to be criticizing what seemed more appropriate in the sixties and seventies. The process of development should be continuous, both within communities and individuals.

We've all met people who have stopped thinking or growing at some point, whether at eighty or thirty years old. I remember, in my early days in Halton, taking the sacrament to the home of two elderly sisters who proudly showed me the new carpet they'd bought, at an age when most people might think the old one would probably see them through. I found that n introducing new ideas about ministry and worship (and the two belong inseparably together), it was quite often the retired or elderly who would consider carefully and then be the first to see the point and give wholehearted support. At parish meetings to learn about and discuss worship one elderly lady would take copious notes and report back to those unable to be there. Fundamentally the parish strategy is the communication, which takes many forms, of whether or not the clergy are really engaged in sharing authority. A parish I know of recently had great difficulty in persuading Parochial Church Council members to pay to go away together for a weekend to discuss parish policy. It wasn't that they couldn't afford the £25: rather, they sensed, quite accurately, that the Vicar had already decided what he wanted and what would be "best" for the people, and that at the end of the weekend he would have his way. It's not worth anyone's time or money to condone fake collegiality, however innocently meant. I am well aware that no one, least of all myself, is free from this accusation; after all, clergy probably spend far more time than is good for them thinking about their parish's life and worship. When we do this we get too far "ahead" of everyone else, and naturally feel impatient when others don't see our great vision in its entirety and immediacy. The apocryphal tale of one parish's transition from the Series 2 Rite to Series 3 is worth telling for the caricature of a frighteningly true-to-life situation. To be fair, the parish in question was one of those rather sad places that have once ministered very strongly but patronizingly to the local streets of back-to-back red brick houses, with their cobbled streets and washing strung from one side to another, but which now are eclectic, gathering a congregation from miles around but saying little about the presence of God to the neighbourhood. In such a church, where the flowers are obviously arranged by the clergy, and the magazine is the product of a single mind, the transition from Series 2 to Series 3 happened like this.

On the Sunday morning in question, the parish priest arrived with a large cardboard box. "Harry," he says to the warden, "please will you put all these new green books out for the service and take all the blue ones round the back of the church and burn them." But such a situation where it exists, whether in mild or extreme form, is a connivance, a game to be played by several players. I recognize, however, how hard it can be when as a parishioner you decide that it is more important to stay with the situation and try gently to change it, rather than to move out and look for somewhere more congenial, or try a house church or just fade out of church life temporarily or for good.

Although I tried hard in Halton to move slowly and to offer plenty of opportunity for everyone to learn and share their new understanding, I did have very positive ideas about what would be helpful for us to pursue. The worship I inherited was an immaculate and orderly ritual, performed by dedicated servers at an Eastward-facing altar a long distance from the congregation. There was nothing surprising in this. It was the moderate tractarian tradition, given that sort of church, having had that sort of history. I felt that it all needed to be a lot more popular and ordinary, so that more types of people could share in it without having first to change and become different people. At heart, it seemed possible for the

110

congregation to attend and observe such worship with great pleasure, but to retain their right to be uninvolved and uncommitted. Of course it was only possible at all because a few very central people, whilst expecting that the majority of the others would not be, were themselves utterly dedicated. Essential points for me were that all are called to pray, in their own way certainly, and not to feel that a few pray while others depend upon them. Also that we had to work at changing the use of words in a book and carefully rehearsed movement into real prayer for everyone, including children and young people.

Over the past ten years the value placed on silence has rapidly gained in importance through the churches. The restful waiting on God, for example after the reading of a lesson or hearing a sermon, or before saying a form of corporate confession, has become commonplace, although it takes a lot of confidence in the one responsible to allow anything like sufficent space to create a positive silence. So often we are constantly promised "silence" by those leading acts of worship, but never actually get any. So called Quiet Days begin late and end early, and are punctuated by the ever-ready rattle of spoons in saucers. Many elderly people avoid retreats and opportunities for silence, on the grounds that they can have as much silence as they want at home every day, for nothing. But there are many who, whether consciously or not, are a little afraid of silence, perhaps because of the commitment implied in taking one's religion seriously. I remember the first occasion when, sitting in the president's chair at the parish communion, I made a silent space after the administration; one regular member of the congregation covered her embarrassment by insisting later that she thought I'd fainted or been taken suddenly ill.

It may be unhelpful to admit it, but we never did resolve one of the perennial problems of the Parish Communion, which is casual chatter beforehand, during and immediately after. Most of us have known on occasions a church where one can hear a pin drop before the mass begins. It was not so with us. Different parishes, I know, stressing how important is silence before the start of any great creative activity, have tackled this sometimes in unique and imaginative ways. I have known clergy who wrote powerful magazine articles on the subject, preached heart-rending sermons, lectured severely and at length in the notices – pointing out that it is during coffee afterwards that all the gossiping is supposed to take place – rang bells at strategic moments, even went to the length of sitting in the president's chair for a full quarter of an hour before the service. The results of all this essentially clerical and patronizing use of energy are severely limited.

The way forward must at least be an honest sharing of the problem with all concerned. Such discussions reveal that not everyone finds silence before the service congenial or appropriate. Some say that they have prepared the readings, their intercessions, confession and thanksgiving at home the previous night. What they need to do on arriving in church is to re-establish their relationships with people whom they may not have seen for a few days. Not all churches have coffee after the service, and people from families that are not all members of the church often feel constrained to rush off immediately after the dismissal to pick up the threads of the family Sunday. Others argue that the Parish Communion is meant to be a joyful and intimate gathering of God's people for a family meal, and it is therefore unnatural to sit in isolated silence beforehand. Such thoughts may seem unreasonable to many for whom silence before the service is precious, but a mature exploration of the whole situation by all concerned is in any event required.

The conclusion – if that is not too strong a word – that I came to in Halton, about stillness before worship, was in two parts. Firstly, that with a daily eucharist which was usually attended by at least half a dozen people (involving altogether, over the week, quite a large number of the Sunday congregation), there was plenty of opportunity for quiet personal devotion for those for whom it had become important. Secondly, given our move from a service which had over-balanced towards being world-denying and ritualistic, to one which was more open to the world, involved families with small children and was less rarified, it was inevitable that there should be some confusion about what kind of behaviour was appropriate by way of preparation. However, the servers were always seen to gather in the apse for five or six minutes of silence, followed by a short form of prayer, before the service began. I always hoped that their careful witness was an encouragement and sign to those in the congregation who were trying to find a few moments' recollection at that point. Indeed, since I left the parish and structural work on the apse made it necessary for a time for this preparation to be in the North transept, right on the edge of the congregation, it had an even more marked influence.

## The Servers

This may be an appropriate moment to say something about the servers, who always provided an essential element in the worship, and were in themselves highly representative of the entire congregation. For no reason that I could justify logically, I never actively encouraged female servers and no one ever seriously applied. We had about twenty boys and men across the age spectrum. It was probably the one contribution to the church's worship which was distinctively theirs to be proud of.

On closer reflection, I can see that it was possible and right to have only male servers because of the complementary circumstances. Firstly, we were moving away from being a church that was largely controlled by men, in that there were women on the Church Council and on several committees

113

who were exercising real authority. Secondly, we had moved the sanctuary into the middle of the church, so that rather than having two "rooms", the sanctuary entirely controlled by men and the nave mostly full of women, the architecture of the church fostered an almost womb-like experience. With people on four sides of the sanctuary, including a small choir behind the altar, with no one more than a few rows of seats from the focus of activity, and with as many people as possible involved in the liturgy, there was an experience of everyone participating, rather than being dominated by a group of men in the sanctuary. Thirdly, we were more open to the movement of the Holy Spirit, renewing our life in Christ through personal prayer, a greater willingness to listen to God and to one another, a commitment to caring for each other and the world. Sister Pia Buxton, IBVM, who concentrates on giving spiritual direction and teaching people to pray, has suggested that many of the signs of hope in the church today are "quite radically feminine". Certainly I believe that I was inviting our servers to share with others the more tender, more approachable side of their nature. For those who could bear to do that (and one or two who were very conscious of their maleness in their work and in the way they ran their families did give up serving under my regime), there was a release of new spiritual energy. Indeed, there was a new quality to their relationships with their wives and women in general. Fourthly, the visual effect of an all-male serving team was balanced by some female presence in the choir, a female organist for much of the time, and one or two women regularly on a rota to assist with the administration of communion.

I was extremely fortunate in that the head server, with fifty years of experience behind him, was able to catch the vision of how the eucharist might be celebrated by everyone present, instead of being a beautiful ritual merely to be witnessed by most of the congregation. The co-operation and leadership of the servers was a vital strand in our movement to modern liturgy. There were early anxieties that these ideas were just my unfortunate idiosyncrasies, and that, in changing from what was well-known and safe to something else, all sense of the the otherness and glory of God would inevitably be lost. In fact, I believe we managed to combine the best of the old with the most helpful and attractive of the new.

What was new were simplified and unfussy movements, the smart efficiency of cassock-albs, a new liturgy based on a Westward-facing nave altar, and the almost undefinable knack of combining formality with informality. The Franciscan Mission team generously described our worship as a combination of catholic dignity and charismatic spontaneity, the feeling of being the Family of God in the presence of a great mystery. Yet we kept the old discipline and careful preparation, the rehearsed movements which are unobtrusive and hardly noticed consciously by the worshippers, and encouraged the servers to regard themselves as a small group with a spiritual life within the congregation. The servers held a monthly evening eucharist, open to all, followed sometimes by a meeting of their own. There is something important here about giving the psychological "permission" to very ordinary working men and schoolboys to take seriously (but not sanctimoniously) their life in Christ. Many of them received spiritual direction and the sacrament of penance. The obvious spiritual calibre of the servers made it possible for those planning worship at major festivals to explore, without creating too much anxiety, a whole range of symbolism, including ashing on Ash Wednesday, an outdoor procession on Palm Sunday, footwashing on Maundy Thursday, veneration of the cross on Good Friday, a dawn vigil and service of light preceding the Holy Communion on Easter Day, the most moving regular baptisms at the Parish Communion, and the occasional dignified but matter of fact use of incense. All that is good and helpful in other traditions can so easily be made use of in worship, given that at its heart lies the integrity and the clear commitment of those involved, displayed in their Christian discipleship.

## The Peace

The sharing of the peace in the parish communion says vital things about Christian concern for the peace of the world. The American Trappist monk, Thomas Merton, once reflected that if a country were to be overrun by a totalitarian government, the first people to be arrested should be the contemplatives. It is those who pray in stillness who are more dangerous than the political act'vists, because they see clearly into the heart of things, recognizing that the only true hope of peace comes from God. Worship loses its essential value when it is regarded as cut off from life. The God to whom we direct our praises has been revealed in Jesus. In recognizing Jesus as the Risen Christ, his disciples were seeing the Messiah who, in his words, miracles of healing, and compassion for the poor and outcast, had revealed God's true nature, as passionately opposed to all that diminishes humankind. In raising Jesus from the dead, the Father was saying "Yes" to all that in his earthly ministry, death and resurrection he had revealed about God's relationship with us. Bishop David Jenkins has told us, in his own inimitable way, that Jesus "came into the midst of fear, frustration and human nonsense. Here was one who was totally for good, for God, and for people". In the man Jesus, his believing disciples recognized at the same time both the disclosure of God and all of humanity that is good, true and whole; Jesus' life, death and resurrection have all to be regarded as one revelation of God's mind and purposes. It was the fact that Jesus was fully alive with God's life, and at the same time took into himself all that was significant and admirable in

116

humanity and lived it through convincingly, against treacherous opposition and without the support of under-standing friends, even to sacrificing his life, that enabled others to recognize him as "the Christ". He was the unique one who could bring God's forgiveness, hope and salvation. In the Resurrection, the Father sets his seal on Jesus' portrayal of what God is like and what he is concerned about, and what humanity at its best can be. In the Resurrection God also sets his face against the suffering and death inflicted by people on Jesus, and on so many millions who have suffered at the hands of others and from disease and fear throughout history. Like Jesus himself, the company of baptized Christians has the commission to reveal God's deep concern for humanity, especially in its poverty and suffering, the crucifixions of every generation: the gas chambers, the Northern Ireland murders, the deaths from cancer and from AIDS, the Zeebrugge tragedy, the various poverty traps of modern society, and not least the hopelessness of long-term unemployment. The content of our hymns, sermons and intercessions should always reflect the understanding of God we have if the Jesus we know from the gospels is God's Son, our Lord and Saviour. The exchange of the peace is a pivotal point of the Parish Communion, and although as you do it you can't possibly have all these ideas in your conscious mind, I believe this to be an essential subconscious and background frame of reference.

One of the basic meanings of sharing the peace is, I believe, to reveal a commitment to creating a Church that is not a ghetto in which to hide away, but a ministering body which, like Jesus Christ, is committed, corporately and through its individual members, to be peacemakers. But we cannot presume to be the teachers or the conscience of the world unless the church's life is itself a paradigm or a symbol of the search for peace. Peace is not merely the absence of conflict but a possible condition for those who in some small way are growing in their relationship with God.

I believe in the fundamental equality of every Christian minister, lay and ordained, because of our common life made possible through baptism into Christ's Body. Within the Church we must all be wanting to be one, regardless of human barriers of race, social standing or wealth. We cannot pick and choose our Christian friends. The Church should be observably the place where you can see how human beings relate to one another when God rules. The Church's inner life is an important seedbed, a place for preparing Christians to become true companions, without condescension, with all. Yet, according to one Franciscan friar who spends much of his time with prisoners and ex-prisoners, when prison chaplains ring up a parish priest to ask if someone coming out into the community again can hope to find support there, they often meet with a reply to the effect that "unfortunately we're not that sort of parish". It was a measure of the openness of our church community that when a member of the congregation was imprisoned for several months, in a quiet way but by quite a number of people who were aware of the circumstances, his wife and family were supported, and later he was received back with hardly any comment. Care was taken not to make life difficult, by protecting him (within the congregation's life) from circumstances that left him open to his particular temptation in the future. Unfortunately, it is one thing for a congregation to tolerate and forgive relatively minor offences, but much more difficult to find a properly Christian attitude of reconciliation towards those found guilty of rape or of violence towards the elderly.

It is in this context that the exchange of the peace within worship should be taken seriously and joyfully. To do so reminds us that the Parish Communion is the church community gathered to break bread together and so to know the presence of Christ. It is not some perfunctory ritual done on our behalf. But I know of people who find the exchange of the peace enormously painful, like one lady in a parish where I was helping out during a vacancy, who recoiled from my proffering of the peace with the words, "No, thank you. I don't have it!" This made me reflect quite irresponsibly (the alternative would be insanity) that, like the modern cinema with part of the seating marked off as a "no smoking" area, perhaps our churches need areas designated as "no peace passed on this side".

Rather than dismissing all such people as awkward, those of us whose ideas about the church happen to be in the ascendancy at the moment might consider the very human reasons why, for some of our neighbours, the peace seems so distasteful. For example, many people prefer to live in homes that are hedged and walled away from others, and they tend to avoid having their personal space invaded unless they can help it. Even visiting the doctor or being admitted to hospital can be a major ordeal, as it involves loss of privacy or personal freedom. There are some who from childhood have either been deprived of or discouraged from the sense of touch, except within a very intimate family circle or in shaking hands on being introduced to a stranger. Of course there is also the straightforward reason that it's human not to want to greet with enthusiasm someone you don't like, don't know by name or whose dog regularly chases your cat up the nearest tree. One churchwarden in a church I was visiting told me in an open way, "We don't pass the peace here because, as you see, there're only seventeen of us and we've all known each other for years. It is not as though there were any strangers to make welcome".

For a number of people, though, the peace is a serious and deep cause of dispute because of what it represents. For these people the peace is symbolic of all that they dread in society and now, unfortunately, even in the church. In society they recognize the breakdown of family life, law and order, and the ordered ways which they recall from their childhood. In the church this is represented by left-wing clerics, liberal bishops who don't give a clear lead on moral issues and don't know what they believe, the demise of the Authorized Version of the Bible and the Book of Common Prayer, the ordination of women, and the promotion of a general mateyness in church life. In point of fact, though they would believe me to be wrong, I regard the exchange of the peace as a crucial symbol of what they are called to be by constantly and carefully doing what Christians are meant to do. In short, among other things, in humility to offer to the world a model of how women and men can live together as companions and with hope when God is allowed to have his way. Although this itself is precisely the point at which many English church people – wanting to be generous and open to the world and fearful of becoming a sect, and probably not entirely confident of burning their boats and totally committing themselves as Christians – would want to call a halt.

The peace is not just a handshake. In fact, in some congregations it has grown into an intricate activity where bearhugs, kisses and tears are regularly exchanged. In Halton, both on Sundays and at daily eucharists, many would move from their seats and greet others: it became a real communication, hand to hand and eye to eye. It was a growth point, especially on significant occasions for the entire community, such as a major festival, a confirmation or after the death of someone known to everyone. And sometimes it would have heightened significance for two individuals or a group concerned with a particular project. Then, with no demeaning of the worship intended or conveyed, the formally provided words of greeting could become instead, "I hope you're recovered"; "I'm sorry about your brother's death"; "Welcome!"; "I forgive you"; "Happy anniversary!"; "Sorry I went off the deep end at the Church Council meeting"; and so on. This was the recognition of the truth that we belong to a people who have God for their Father and therefore everyone else as brother or sister. Certainly the existence of peace in the church is not automatic, and the more lay people are involved and many take on responsibilities, the more ways there are for people to get hurt. But passing the peace is to state that we depend for our common salvation, not on our cleverness, busyness or commitment, but on the sacrifice of Christ's death on the cross. Only the risen power of Christ, which brought the experience of peace and forgiveness to the disciples in the upper room, can help us. It is that peace which we put on the agenda to be received and worked out in our daily lives. I recognize as I take your hand that I am not the centre of the universe; God has as much love and care for you as he does for me. I recognize that living as a Christian community, as in any family, has its ups and downs. I am glad that we can trust one another sufficiently to speak the truth in love, and to keep on offering and receiving mutual forgiveness and encouragement. It will not stop there, because a community that is learning to offer reconciliation to its own members will be increasingly able and willing to share that with the wider world.

## Sharing Responsibility for Worship

In sermons and at planning meetings, my assumption was always that for committed church members worship is an active rather than a passive experience. As far as possible the Development Group for the Church Council took responsibility for looking ahead and making plans for worship. An open invitation usually meant that the regular hymn-choosing meeting was a balance between clergy and laity, both those who were and who were not publicly responsible for the music. With the help of a pile of hymn books, a couple of published guides as to which hymns obviously fit the Sundays of the year, the ASB readings, and eventually our own collected hymn supplement, the hymn-planning meeting could be both an opportunity for some informal teaching and a good degree of hilarity. Those members of the congregation who didn't care for the choice of hymns were often reminded that the hymn-choosing meetings were open to all.

Like most churches, we had a team of faithful and caring people who took it in turns to read and to lead intercessions at the Parish Communion. The rota was administered entirely by the laity without reference to me. The intercessors met regularly for support and instruction. Once a year the readers met in church, and everyone read a passage to the others while one of the clergy or an invited visitor offered constructive criticisms. But the responsibility for the hearing of the Word in church lies with the whole congregation. Listening is not a passive experience. Whereas I tend to feel that lots of lesson-finding immediately before and even during the reading itself is a distraction and a barrier to real attention, it is the responsibility of everyone to have pondered on the readings before they ever arrive in church. We expect the reader of the lesson and the clergy who will preach to have carefully considered the passage beforehand. Any serious member of the congregation, with the aid of their own ASB, lectionary, or weekly notice sheet, can find out what is to be read on any particular Sunday. No one must "go to church" as though to the cinema, expecting to be switched on by the eloquence or dynamic personality of the vicar. There are clergy who run their Parish Communions and family services almost like music halls, and to an extent they are "successful" in that there are some who respond and enjoy their rather eccentric vicar. But we all know what happens to such a situation when he moves or retires. An entertained congregation is dependent, and not a corporate ministering or missionary agency. Besides, we all no doubt remember the old story of the elderly lady leaving church with her young and perceptive niece after a Sunday morning service. In response to the lady's grumbling about the cold church, the choice of hymns, and the sermon, the niece replies, "Well, auntie, what do you expect for fifty pence?" This is not so much a comment about the paucity of most people's giving to the church, as about the expectation of most members of congregations that it is the vicar's show and it had better be good.

Baptism into the Body of Christ makes us all equally responsible for the quality of the celebration of the eucharist. We all have different parts to play, both in the total ministry of the congregation and the specific acts of a piece of worship. Only a few are invited to preach, because of their particular gifts. The same is true of the leading of the worship, the reading of lessons, the leading of intercessions and so on, but no one is excused some responsibility, according to their lights, for making a positive contribution by truly listening, singing from the heart, taking a full part with alertness. Not that the eucharist in some way depends for its effectiveness on our contribution. Of course not. It is Christ's death and Resurrection we remember before the Father, knowing that Christ's once-for-all sacrifice is our only strength and hope. But our active response is called for. All of us need to attend with care, having prepared the readings, the intercessions, the penitence, the thanksgiving as well as if we ourselves were to be the president. One server with long experience, who was far from certain at first whether to trust this collaborative ministry talk, tried for a long time to get me to offer the security of being just like my predecessor, though without reckoning on my patient stubbornness. "Father," he said with an expectant glint in his eye, "in the last vicar's time, if I ever turned up to serve with a dirty alb, he would send me home." "Stephen," I replied, "I should expect you to be as concerned as I am that the service will be to God's glory. So the question of your turning up with a dirty alb will not arise."

*

123

# Face to Face with God

Some people approach God at the Parish Communion as though they had been at school with him, while others can only approach with extreme apprehension and always on their knees. I encouraged lots of standing, for those who could manage it, because it reflects an aspect of our relationship with God that we had forgotten, and which we need as a basis for confidence in sharing ministry: namely, that God has created us in his image and he loves us. He assures us that we are very good, even if very good sinners. Because of the crucifixion and resurrection, we can stand among God's people with the confidence that we are redeemed and have a right to be there. Yes, of course there is room for penitence and for growing in discipleship, but no need for constant grovelling. When I was a young boy at church with a couple of school friends, we got the opposite impression. We felt that as long as we kept our heads down below the top of the pew and didn't whisper too loudly, no one would notice us. There is a danger that in subtle and unconscious ways we still mentally promote that among adults. Recently I sat in the nave of a church as a member of a congregation, a rare experience for a priest. Immediately I reacted against the pews. They were designed with a cripplingly sharp overhang behind the shoulders of anyone of more than average height. I reflected on how many groups of men and women had been kept in a mental and physical state of subservience and irresponsibility by such furniture. Certainly I was always thankful that in Halton the original builders had given us light wooden chairs that could be moved and arranged at will. Sometimes the whole or part of the floor space could be cleared for a children's festival, a play or the Easter Vigil. Although storage was a problem, it was worth tackling to be able to have available only approximately the number of chairs likely to be needed for a service, so that people sat together and therefore participated in the worship as a community and with their whole personality.

As I have said earlier, a cynic might argue that in arranging for a nave altar on a dais that was an extension of the choir floor level, we had simply exchanged the throne room of an Eastern Potentate for a modern hall set out for a shareholders' meeting. But the way we worship is not accidental or incidental. Our religious experiences are the direct result of what we do and how we do it. This means that we must take the trouble to worship God in ways that are true to our understanding of him and our relationship with him. There is such a danger that in any age our worship, our buildings, our forms of liturgical speech, get trapped in a time capsule. So often in the Church of England we feel constrained to use other people's prayers, previous generations' architectural genius, and former generations' translations of the scriptures, instead of daring, like Jesus himself, to come close to God as "Abba" and therefore to communicate with him directly and with honesty in our contemporary ways.

## The Importance of a Suitable Worship Space

We can detect that at the heart of early Christianity lay the worship of God in Trinity, Father, Son and Holy Spirit. Down the generations the Church has been the Church it was and realized its mission essentially through the way it has worshipped. So many local churches today cannot come to be what their ideas and aspirations hope for because of the burden of tradition in their buildings. They are weighed down with history, even if their church was only designed and erected in the last century. It is partly, I'm sure, because we hardly dare give importance to our feelings and physical relationships, believing that words are what really matter. Yet we know from the human sciences that over seventy per cent of human interchange goes beyond words, and we all accept traditional wisdom such as "Actions speak louder than words".

I am making a plea for us to be less hampered by our buildings. Large choirs are so rare these days, they lead better from within the congregation anyway, and many churches have a variety of music groups that don't robe. Here is the opportunity to remove the choir stalls in many churches and use that whole area for a sanctuary, with the priest having a seat in which to preside over the worship, thus allowing as many to participate as possible, as he increasingly does in the day-to-day life of the parish. A growing number of courageous congregations, with the help of sensitive architects who are often so generous with time and resources, have re-ordered their whole church building, making the best use of all available space. To do so whole-heartedly is not a luxury nor merely cosmetic, because it both states what sort of community they believe they are becoming and enables them to be more able to make progress in that direction. May their numbers increase!

Again, the theology we have of God should be reflected in the physical ways we share in worship. For example, we know that God has shared our life in Jesus and is in our midst when two or three gather together, and that he shares the powerlessness of so much human ordinariness and suffering. We know too that all God's people are equally called to service, though a minority have the extra call to priesthood. There are so many powerful theological ideas that we could help ourselves to *feel more deeply* if we only took care in the arrangement of the church buildings, took care not to be too remote from ordinary life by putting on special churchy voices for worship or by dressing up lay people to play the organ, sing in the choir, or administer Holy Communion. Again, we should reveal that the eucharistic prayer is a unified process of taking, blessing, breaking and sharing the bread by adopting a single bodily position throughout, rather than kneeling at the Words of Institution. We could *feel* that we are a redeemed, hopeful and ministering body by standing together in confidence to receive the bread and the wine. By contrast, especially at weekday services, the physical setting often gives the impression that clergy and people belong in separate rooms, at different floor levels, that the congregation are not one corporate people, and are often acutely uncomfortable in chapels whose designs reflect the spirituality and theology of those early years of this century, when only the tractarian movement had any confidence to give guidance about how church interiors should be designed.

Amidst all the reactionary lobbies of those who are most concerned to preserve our national heritage, we need to state quite boldly that theological and liturgical principles must be the churches' first consideration. Every new generation of Christians has the duty to make its best and considered contribution to the continuing Tradition, rather than be threatened so much by the past that it is afraid to do what it needs to do in the present. I am not suggesting that congregations should be cultural philistines, or that we do not experience the creative presence of God through ancient buildings, with their sense of wonder and transcendence. Rather, it is a matter of balanced discernment.

Today we are wanting to express that our eucharistic worship, the heart of all that makes us the Church, is not a ritualistic action beautifully presented by a handful of people in a separate room within the church, on behalf of the majority of passive onlookers, also in their own room. Our theology is that we are sharing in a communion meal with Christ our Lord at the centre. *All* of us are celebrating with equal responsibility, though the clergy will be holding it all together and representing the apostolic faith in and for the whole community, as they do in the church's ministry. If this is the theology and the liturgical experience we believe in principle we should rightfully be promoting, we have a responsibility to bring it about, to make it happen, to let people *experience* it. The words of worship are only a part of the total experience, and what we provide in terms of architecture, furniture, lighting, acoustics and the way our whole persons, including our bodies, relate to one another, is a vital element. For those who lead worship to be able to use differing speeds and volume of speech at various times and still be heard, and to have eyeball contact with everyone, seems to me to be essential.

There are so many congregations whose worship is flat and timid, partly because they are not taking their courage in both hands and remoulding their church as a good room in which to celebrate the liturgy. Dwindling choirs in choir stalls often prevent a real communication between nave and sanctuary. Many Church Councils have eased the altar a few inches away from the East Wall so that the vicar can squeeze in and face the people, whereas a much more radical change would be much more helpful. So many choir stalls could actually be placed elsewhere or removed from the building altogether, allowing for the present tiny sanctuaries to be remodelled in the whole of the area presently occupied by choir stalls. The absence of altar rails, the creation of solid-looking altars that are nevertheless movable, the resiting of the organ, making floors warm and comfortable to the feet and for children to sit on, and the replacement of pews by substantial yet movable chairs, are all possible elements to be looked at in recreating church buildings for worship in accord with the main thrust of present-day eucharistic theology. Some choir areas and sanctuaries are so narrow that they would be best made into small chapels, separated with perhaps a glass screen or a dramatic drop of fabric which can be seen through but acts as a barrier, so that such chapels can be independently heated. Increasingly I believe that *all* celebrations of the eucharist, even when just a handful of people gather during the week, are essentially communal and public rather than primarily private and devotional. The way the furniture is arranged, and therefore how priest and people relate physically to one another, has the power either to affirm and build upon this or to deny it.

A congregation needs to spend time working out what its theology of the eucharist is, and this may lead to a more or less common consent that the nave could be entirely re-thought, perhaps even with the new sanctuary on the longer North or South side, or in the centre, as appropriate. We shall always have to work round medieval monuments, Jacobean screens, eighteenth-century sounding boards, and the whole business of the invisible strings tied to memorial gifts, but these should not in themselves allow us to lose heart. The most central theological truth that we are learning today is that the Church is a communion of people in Christ and that we live in this communion, modelled on the life of the Trinity itself, without the implication that anyone is subordinate to another. There are many, I know, who consider that a great deal of fuss about the arrangement of the church furniture is irrelevant, and that words on their own say all that is necessary. Furthermore, those who are opposed to major re-ordering are not convinced by the primary claims of theological principle, even if they accept the contemporary understanding of the eucharist on which I have based my argument. The primacy of how much all this is going to cost is far more likely to persuade.

Yet those who claim to love their parish churches "as they have always been" have clearly not studied the plans of the building at various times over the past few hundred years. I found one parish priest with re-ordering on his mind, busy photocopying such church plans from the eighteenth and nineteenth centuries to show to his Church Council exactly how much those different generations had contrasting visions of the way the church needed to be, and had gone about putting them into practice. And then there are those who put great stress on how much they love the old church and wouldn't have a stone touched, who may not be the most regular of attenders, while the worshipping congregation itself, especially those who are there during the week, may have a burning desire to make the building a more effective vehicle of God's presence for today. Again, some of these churches that are supposed to be so precious to our national heritage are starved of love and the financial resources needed to care for them properly. Although many Church Councils work very hard to maintain their churches, some are kept in a very poor state, allowed to get dry rot, not properly heated, with drains full of grass, repairs left undone, relics of old furnishings and projects piled in corners, and frequently not very clean. Some churches look so sad, as if they have just given up.

I had an example of this conflict between "love" of the old place and the contemporary needs of the church in my own parish, when we first thought of re-ordering the nave. There were some red curtains across the entrance to the two transepts. When the architects' plans were revealed to the congregation, there were cries of horror that those lovely old curtains, given in memory of a former pillar of the church, would have to come down. And apart from that, what a draught there would be! On closer examination, the curtains were found to be absolutely filthy, no one having expressed their "love" for them by taking them to the dry cleaners. Unfortunately, when we did, at the insistence of the Church Council, they disintegrated completely.

When parishioners start sending petitions to the Archdeacon, complaining that the new Rector is wanting to remove the gates from their ancient rood screen, I seriously wonder whether we are living in the same church. Clergy certainly do need the wisdom to teach carefully and to share all thinking before making rash and insensitive statements about ancient buildings, although one hears of anxieties about "time-honoured" furniture these days that is barely forty years old. And again, responsible members of Church Councils and congregations should be more willing to listen to the ideas of their priests, hopefully representing to them the collective wisdom of the wider Church.

Although the ancient churches carry our history with them, they do have the primary function of facilitating our relationship with God and with each other in communion with him, and we should never allow anyone, no matter how powerful or strident their voice, to lose sight of that. This is, in fact, a reminder that in all our talk of encouraging the laity to have their proper say and share in church life, we are not talking about a complete parallel with modern democracy. The parish priest has a vital role of teaching and leading each successive generation into new truths, provided it is done *from within* rather than *over against* the whole Church.

I am convinced that a very important part of the process of reclaiming the Church involves reclaiming our buildings from the anxieties of archaeologists, antiquarians and conservationists. We must reclaim church buildings from the lack of theological insight, lack of an excited vision of the local church's mission, lack of financial generosity, and from the apathy that fails to recognize the significance of the way in which our physical surroundings either support or negate our contemporary understandings of the spiritual journey.

## Worship and Openness to the World

The understandings of a single congregation vary, of course. While some speak of God as friend, lover or companion, others feel happier with God kept in a more formal relationship, and dub rather too quickly as "charismatic" any less formal or emotional approach to worship. Yet in our parish life in Halton, I found that by deliberately offering the celebration of the eucharist in different styles on various occasions, many people could be gently given a deeper and more intimate relationship with God. The experiences that result make it worth all the trouble to fill the church with candles and no other lights at Christmas midnight, to celebrate the eucharist in a simple fashion in a farmhouse kitchen on a parish holiday, to be a Christian family at home with God in the Parish Communion in many moods, to fill the place with incense on Easter morning, to accompany the mass with an informal music group with all the small children given percussion instruments at a mission service; these are some of the ways in which we can allow parishes to grow in their appreciation of God's incarnational and reconciling presence in the eucharist, without necessarily losing out on the mystery and awe that are equally essential.

I know there are those who are anxious about the loss of our great cultural heritage, and who mourn the loss of the security and beauty of the old forms of worship, with their ordered grace and coherence. Yet we must decide whether we are radically committed to knowing Christ as our contemporary source of salvation or whether we are, instead, hanging on to the Christ of some particular cultural scene of the past. The Church can only hope to be effectively missionary if it is enabling as many people as possible to share in the life of God as they are now, rather than first having to change their culture. A church community is not a place in which to hide away from life's traumas, but one in which we can begin to face up to them in the hope which only a close encounter with the God who was uniquely revealed in the life, death and resurrection of Jesus Christ can provide. Our worship, drawing on all the best of the past: ceremonial, music, songs, words, architecture, must then be reaching forward to the future and accepting the present moment. For us in Western Europe in the late 1980s this is bound to involve, at least for part of our worship, halting gestures, rough-hewn speech and stammering phrases. Although we are perfectly confident that we are upheld and in close touch with the mystery we name God, ours are not the times of triumphalism, complacency or strident confidence. Knowing and worshipping Christ's presence within the darkness of our world, still remembering the horrors of the holocaust and living under the shadow of nuclear war, amidst urban decay and rural decline, and in the full awareness that a radical re-ordering of the world's economic life must at some point be inevitable as the shift in the balance of power moves from the Northern to the Southern hemisphere, requires that our words and symbols must be to some extent elusive and fragmentary. Our hope is not in a God who is "out there" and who controls us like a puppet master, and our worship needs to reflect this. In plain words, our Parish Communion needs to show the marks of suffering and the awareness that on the personal and corporate levels we are living in an uncomfortable world. It is still possible, even with a Parish Communion that attempts to reflect the true situation in which we live, to contain order, dignity, glory, stillness and awe. But as it is the single most important element of the congregation's life each week, the Parish Communion deserves time given to planning, rehearsing, arranging the furniture and so on, in order to bring out the themes and atmosphere inherent in the words.

Younger people, at least, will only belong to a church today because it means something in the context of the life they have to live, gives them dignity and hope, brings them an experience of salvation, not out of duty, habit or respectability. Where such experiences are taking place, you can usually discover a strongly glowing fire centred on worship which, while recognizing the reality of the world in which all of us have to find our salvation, can claim to see the Lord, if only by flickering and uncertain light. And that is why so many of the modern songs among all denominations, like this one from the Taizé community, speak so clearly to our hearts:

In the Lord I'll be ever thankful,
In the Lord I will rejoice!
Look to him, do not be afraid:
In him rejoicing: the Lord is near.

# 9

# Monday Morning Ministry

In recent decades there has been growing interest and enthusiasm for encouraging all the baptized to respond to the call to share in parish-based ministry: visiting, preparing new members for initiation, concern for music and worship. All this is very exciting and important, but we are in danger of forgetting that for the majority of Christians, the place where they will exercise their ministry and witness for Christ will be in their daily lives in the family, in school, at work, in the neighbourhood or in their leisure activities. Certainly we need a confident Church with clear goals, but never at the expense of abandoning the world by drawing all Christians inside for a semi-monastic life and spirituality.

Looking back now to when I was vicar of a parish, with a struggling congregation concentrating on building up a collaborative ministry, I recognize how difficult I found it to hear some church members say firmly that their daily work required all their thought and energy and involvement. In fact, I am now coming to see that our vision has to be large enough to give the majority of members of congregations the freedom to celebrate their Monday Morning Ministry.

Inevitably most of the recent important encouragement for every baptized person to see themselves as having a ministry has developed with a strong bias towards church-centredness. We now have a special responsibility to consider again how leaders within Christian communities can continue to build up and nurture a strong centre, but at the same time promote the notion that discipleship for most people takes place within the ordinary structures of secular society:

In the interactions of their families and friends;
In the neighbourhood;
In people's jobs, whether in the "caring professions"
    or some other;
In their unemployment or retirement;
In their politics, social clubs, trade unions,
    and sports and leisure activities.

Of course this is not a new idea, but it has been overlooked for a time. We need to ask searching questions about the relationship between church life and life in the world, between persons viewed as parishioners and the same persons viewed as dustmen, secretaries or doctors. And to what extent is it true that they are helped by regular membership of their local church to make the vital connection between Christian faith and their every-day responsibilities?

It is all too easy to regard a doctor who attends church on Sunday as a Christian layman out in the world on Monday, almost as if she or he were on the end of a long piece of elastic; as though the church, rather than the surgery, were the centre of the doctor's world. Probably such a view arises naturally enough in the clerical mind because ordained ministers are so much involved with the institution, the worship, the committees, the maintenance of the plant, the continued existence of the churchly presence, the survival of the church in a given place, rather than with mission in all its forms.

Jesus spoke much about the Kingdom of God; that is, the challenging image of what it means for God to rule in the world in every detail of its life. Therefore the doctor in his surgery is concerned with furthering the purposes of God through the exercise of his professional role. The work of the Kingdom is his focus through the work of healing. Simply drumming up trade for the Church could be a dangerous distraction from the doctor's important and unique task. His or her role will involve helping patients to face many subtle ethical decisions, for example about contraception among teenagers and the abortion of unwanted pregnancies. The doctor's opportunities for witnessing silently to his or her Christian faith come, for example, in times of crisis where it would be so easy to be detached and offer scientific help. Although it's true that many a non-Christian doctor could be relied upon to go the extra mile in terms, say, of sitting a long while in silence with someone in shock or giving generously of his time to a patient hysterical with grief after a tragedy, we should look to a Christian doctor to be in the forefront of such caring. It would be more the task of a Christian GP to add half an hour on to the end of surgery regularly just to listen to someone who is lonely or sad, rather than to be in a rush to get to a Church Council meeting. At the very least a Christian should be expected to give good value to his employer and patients, rather than cutting corners to be busy with parish affairs. Though this is not to say we should not look to a Christian doctor to help with a marriage preparation group if he felt called in that direction. Perhaps the central point is that he should feel free to make his working day the principal place of his ministry, without having to resist undue pressure from his parish priest to be involved in the church's activities. I have used the doctor as an example, but it is perfectly possible and right to apply the principle to others. The Church has a natural empathy with those in caring or teaching roles, spending other people's money, and knows how to minister to them from long experience. However, when it comes to ministering to and with those who create wealth, that's another matter entirely, in which Christian leaders on the whole have little expertise. Those who work in industry, commerce and government certainly face complex issues. Yet the clergy are more likely to criticize from the sidelines in pressure groups and sermons, supporting someone working in the field of promoting healthy family life or the good of the local community simply because that is what they mostly understand best.

I know how often I have been guilty, sometimes unconsciously, of labelling as "less committed" those who feel unable to take a strong part in the round of parish activities. That returns us to the question: "What primary loyalty should we be encouraging – the Church or the Kingdom?" How often we forget that the two are not the same. I see the truth partly in that clergy are more protected from some of the harsh realities of life like house-buying and ownership, ethical decisions at work, or a genuine, unprotected relationship with a wide range of types of people. Far more than the official representatives of the Church, many members of our congregations are called to be God's witnesses in many difficult, ambiguous and spiritually dangerous human situations. To slam more and more guilt for not getting involved in the church on to busy people who cannot take any more by Friday night, is a recipe for a crisis in a marriage or a split with the church. Young adults especially, because they are generally few in number in the church, often are over-worked in Sunday Schools, Youth Clubs, and on the Church Council. We get the balance wrong, forgetting the sensitive claims of their family life, and their need to be nourished by teaching and experience of prayer rather than wrongly committing all their leisure time to the church's machinery, whether of management or evangelism. I have known people who are at church when they ought to be facing up to tasks at work or at home. It is a serious thing to be at services or committee meetings when in fact Christian love demands that you try to resolve conflicts with colleagues, or take responsibility for the upbringing of your children, or work for a deeper relationship with your spouse. There is part of the priest's job which is to say firmly to some people that they should not volunteer for more church work because they owe it to their families or their employers to be more engaged with them. The same could be true of politics, locally and nationally. Christian communities should be producing men and women who see the political or community arena as a very relevant, though tough, environment for working out their vocation in Christ's service. I would like to follow Luther in saying that in every field of human endeavour Christians can experience God's call to service, though with the steady rise in long-term unemployment, it becomes difficult to be glib about a vocation for all.

I fell into the trap of many clergy in small or precarious parishes, of working for the building up of the church, frequently at the expense of the development of the full life of its members. I know now how my whole-hearted pursuit of collaborative ministry left some very busy people feeling guilty because they were torn between giving time to parish, home and work. As a counter-balance, we need to find strong ways of affirming all church members in their particular paths of discipleship, especially where these paths take them very far from the church's life and experience. We need to bring more about Monday Morning into the worship on Sunday. So often clergy and laity conspire in the ghetto mentality that leaves cares and responsibilities at the church door. Not long ago, I heard a priest haranguing a Church meeting, telling the people to let the world get on with its noisy racket and press on instead with the search for holiness. In one way, he was quite right in that he pleaded, with heavy support from R.S. Thomas, George Herbert and Metropolitan Anthony Bloom, for the church to be more "holy". If we were "more holy", he said, the world would take notice and we might even get persecuted. There is, it is true, an important part of Christianity that is to do with withdrawal, solitude and waiting on God in the silence. I'm not denying that; I do it myself as often as I can. I hope I would always be sure to encourage all Christians to cultivate regular stillness, to go on retreats, and to be glad of our great heritage of hermits, contemplatives and all the great teachers of prayer and the presence of God. But our spirituality cannot be helpful to those majority of Christians if it is essentially monastic rather than engaged in depth and at risk in the world's nonsense and frustrations. The danger is that we present ourselves to the world as despising the hustle and bustle of business, decision-taking, protesting, wealth-creating, community-building and so on. Certainly we must be godly, continually sharing in the life of God, but this also involves hard thinking, time-consuming involvement on committees, doing a day's work, taking responsibility for the sort of world we're creating, and trying to reveal some sort of hope from God in a world that is often bleak, evil and apparently Godless.

Certainly people ought to reject a church that is never still or open to receiving God's peace. The more common problem, however, is that it so often looks to the outsider that his or her human culture is being repudiated by Christians who don't want to get their hands dirty, or that the Church is like one of those gentlemen's clubs of *Punch* cartoons where everyone has fallen asleep or *rigor mortis* may actually have set in without anybody noticing or clearing away the remains.

How easy it is to hold a Harvest Thanksgiving or a Mothering Sunday service that is rich in stirring hymns, nostalgia and cosy sentimentality but impoverished in challenge about life styles or social and political issues. A bunch of flowers on Mothering Sunday, a pious sermon about Motherhood, and all the men generously and with much mirth washing up, is a poor substitute for a shared approach to bringing up the children and the giving of proper dignity to women in family, work and church life, or proper concern for the fight for economic justice in the developing nations. It is not insignificant that it was only as Britain began to change from being essentially an agrarian society to an urban industrial one that Church Harvest Thanksgiving began to take on an important part in the annual church cycle. The Church lives on the knife-edge balance of becoming one big nostalgia racket replete with thirteenth-century sedelia, the Book of Common Prayer, matching the pure brown bread and cocoa of the make-believe 1930s television adverts and the golden age of English respectability in the televised Agatha Christie novels. At a practical level, how many congregations have any idea just what pressures and responsibilities in the wider world are represented among their number? How often do church intercessions really reach out to important issues in people's lives?

Some, perhaps most, clergy are so anxious about holding a small congregation together, that they find it difficult to risk asking political and economic questions about the relationship between the world of work and the faith, except in very bland terms. In order to be able to do this we need to create opportunities to listen to those laity who really are involved in and have reflected on issues that we know little of at first hand. There are many clergy nowadays who have worked several years in secular employment before ordination and who also take seriously their role of parenting. Besides this we could make more use of the many non-stipendiary ministers (NSMs) who have a foot in both camps. But as yet the Church as a whole, and parish clergy in particular, have not sorted out the role of the NSM, and many are transferring all the time to the stipendiary ministry, partly because they are misunderstood or overused. Very few NSMs, it seems, are able to regard their priestly vocation as primarily exercised at their place of work.

I found that if I stopped talking and being busy in order to listen carefully to lay people, there was often revealed a layer of scepticism or aggression about church beliefs, in the light of their work and home experiences, that can be hard for clergy to handle. There are many, of course, who want church to be a fantasy, an escape world, a bolt-hole from the cold winds of economics and family stress. Others may need an update on their concept of God and our relationship with him expressed in the Bible and in our prayers. Do most church leaders have to leave it to the David Jenkinses of the Church to be scapegoats, while the rest keep our heads and voices down and plough a less ambitious and less challenging furrow?

We cannot do that because we have been charged with giving vision and responsibility to God's front-line troops. Instead of regarding the laity as "helpers" of the clergy, the notion must be turned on its head, and clergy be taught to understand that they are in fact commissioned to be "helpers" of the laity. Their task in so many ways is to give vision and encouragement to the whole Church, themselves included, to be an agent of God's Kingdom. In the course of the preparations for the 1987 Synod on the Laity, Cardinal Hume expressed this succinctly:

> It is very important to make clear to them [meaning all Christians living in the secular world, priests as well as laity] that the vocation and role of the laity is to be found principally in the conscientious discharge of their family responsibilities, in the conduct of their daily lives at work and in society. It is here through their integrity, their sense of justice and fairness, their kindliness and concern, that they will make their surroundings a little more human, decent and welcoming. Society may not seem to be sanctified or transformed to any remarkable degree

by lives like these, but then we recall Christ's own description of the Kingdom as mustard seed and leaven.

Lecture at All Hallows College, Dublin
20th September 1986

The laity go daily where professional ministers only occasionally go and then only with permission. So the worship and the learning activities and the whole thinking of parishes should emphasize and make possible the development of an adult and committed laity. In many cases, committed laity have found that the nourishment of their parish was a diet that needed supplementing by an extra-parochial spiritual movement. In one way that is healthy for them. But what about the majority of lay people who have to rely on their parish alone, and the thousands who have left because the faith they were being offered failed to touch them where their pain was, failed to answer the questions they were perhaps unconsciously asking, about their jobs and their lives? There are so many insights into worship, private prayer, Bible study, living more simply, concern for the development of the world's resources, springing from movements outside the parish and diocese. The renewal movements such as Focolare, Spring Harvest, Cursillo, The Third Order of St Francis, Lee Abbey, Taizé and Julian Groups are helping many to go back to their parishes and bring the problems of work and home life under the Christian microscope, and to place the anxieties of nuclear war and AIDS on the church community's normal agenda. More and more we are freed from the anxiety about what denomination a helpful idea or style has emerged from. Rather than importing any one of these sources of inspiration, hook, line and sinker, clergy need to be helped to learn that with sensitivity they can draw on particular elements at various times, which can enrich the tradition of a congregation worked out in the past. No one expects glib answers; we are aware that issues are not black and white. We can't, for example, simply use the Bible or the words of the Pope as a quarry for solutions. But we are only just at the threshold of the process of stimulating women and men in so many ordinary occupations to make a genuine connection between their belief in and experience of God, and the daily pressure of work and family.

# 10

# Right Judgement

The unwritten, unspoken parish mandate has to permit the president a degree of undemocratic initiative-taking, on occasion, to make critical assessments of the performance of individuals or groups within the community. Often the community has to trust the priest's capacity to exercise right judgement. The reverse side of the coin is the priest's responsibility to articulate and to rejoice in what others are achieving, often against the odds, and to stimulate them to further horizons.

On becoming a parish priest instead of being an assistant, I discovered that you were suddenly left with a more or less open diary, with complete freedom to spend your time as you think best. The way a priest manages his time is, I believe, a key to the matter of sound judgement. Whereas I respect and have tried to live the model of priesthood that demands a sacrificial offering of one's whole life to God, there are good reasons for placing against this a word of caution. The first point I would make is to do with the priest's need to be seen as balancing his vocation to ordination with that to marriage and parenthood, or, if he is not married, to the proper development of his own personal life.

Theological colleges during this century have produced many first rate, highly committed and professional priests who have given their all to the people committed to their charge. One of my predecessors in Halton was a brilliant example. A tremendous mystique arose around such figures.

Ernie Southcott, when he was Vicar of Halton, was said hardly to need any sleep, would still be visiting in the parish late at night, was rarely seen to have time off with his wife and children. Indeed, the saying goes that on the day he was to be interviewed for the post of Provost of Southwark, the whole parish knew something was afoot, because Ernie and his wife had been spotted, dressed up, travelling together on the tram down into town.

Without being any less committed to the word "priesthood", a shift in understanding is making itself felt among younger clergy, though not without some anxiety among those more senior, who are uneasy about being too organized over time off or setting guidelines about the length of a clerical working week. Indeed, it can be taken to extremes, with a few clergy refusing to open their doors or answer the phone on their "day off", and the laity responding by claiming that *they* never have any time off. For a priest to be able to make time to do the garden, take the children swimming, or clean the car, despite the ribbing of neighbours with a more orderly working week, is a sign of confidence and maturity in ministry. And this needs to be encouraged by bishops and congregations. It could be asked of anyone who regularly over-works. "What are you escaping from in the rest of your life?" How many clergy marriage break-downs are the direct result of confusion and lack of self-esteem which leads to being unable to take time off without guilt? Unmarried clergy also need to be encouraged to take seriously their own personal development outside the work in the parish. I shall discuss later some of the issues involved when more than one priest work together in a parish team, but here I just want to make the point that some newly ordained bachelor deacons and priests need help in working out what proportion of the week is appropriate for them to be working. With one of the curates who worked with me in Halton, who is unmarried, I came to realize just how much those of us who are married depend on our wives taking the major responsibility for shopping and maintenance of the household, even combined with voluntary or salaried work of her own, to permit us the freedom to work very long hours, six days a week. A bachelor priest or an unmarried woman deacon should be positively encouraged to see that they owe it to themselves, without guilt, to give time to their social life, homes, gardens, washing and cooking. Church leaders offer a more helpful witness to the nature of God and his dealings with his people when they come over as normal rather than obsessive or eccentric human beings.

There can be no progress towards true baptismal equality while some of us over-work and, however obliquely, imply that others are less committed or dedicated to God's task. Most conscientious clergy readily admit that the social life they enjoyed before ordination, and above all their ability to have friendships outside church circles, are almost impossible to maintain. It is so true that even if clergy and senior laity work eighteen hours a day, we can never do for someone else their own proper share of Christ's ministry. The essential points are, I believe, that no one can effectively do the same job seven days a week – which has good Old Testament support – and that the way we are seen to handle other commitments in our lives, such as marriage, offer profound signals to our congregations about our wholeness and fitness to preside over a church community.

The reasons why clergy do not always take proper holidays are various. They include the fact that some churchwardens and councils just do not have the confidence or the wisdom to encourage their clergy to go on holiday (and, for that matter, on retreats and conferences), not just for their own sakes but for everyone else's too. Clergy with three or four young children and a car to run have financial problems finding somewhere to go on holiday; some are not yet paid or feel able to negotiate for reasonable but realistic expenses of office.

Although some Rural Deans are exemplary in getting holiday cover arranged in very good time, some clergy are just so disorganized or self-sacrificing (at their family's expense) that by the time they get round to planning a holiday they cannot find a clear fortnight or anyone to stand in for them on a Sunday, and end up either staying at home or coming back on Saturday evening to take Sunday services. There are strong grounds for a parish occasionally reducing the number of Sunday services, or stimulating laity to plan them, to ensure that clergy have holidays. In fairness to the so often under-estimated laity, there can be few congregations who would not see the logic of that.

The colleges also gave to many generations of priests a secure foundation in daily prayer, though it was essentially monastic and could serve the once very common young unmarried curate very well. I found it was very difficult to adapt this expectation to the situation of being married with three young children, when the conflict of loyalties between saying the office, changing nappies and taking a sick child to the doctor have to be balanced. One of the greatest helps to me in the parish was to share the saying of parish prayers with groups of lay people and letting them take a full part in the leading, reading and praying. We began to say the Sunday evening office, sitting in a circle of chairs in the Lady Chapel, focusing the eyes on a cross, icon or lighted candle. Regulars joined a rota to say the office, read lessons and lead prayers. We sang hymns unaccompanied. This provided a strong and moving experience, even though the numbers were never high.

A second thread to this development of the office as the corporate and public prayers of the congregation, rather than as the private prayers of the clergy, was to extend the Sunday pattern through the week. There always had been one or two highly committed lay people who had joined the clergy to say the weekday offices, but we developed it, particularly in the evening, as an open and public act of worship. Often extra people would join the regular nucleus before a committee meeting in church, meeting in someone's home. On Saturday evening the emphasis was on preparing for the Sunday eucharist, sometimes with a simple and informal benediction, including a short address, without lots of ceremonial and clutter, but perhaps with incense left to burn beside the altar.

Whenever we had a children's day (as many parishes now do in Holy Week or One World Week), where there would be painting, model making, instrument making, singing, teaching, baking, acting, and so on, we ended with an act of worship. Part of our way of re-ordering the nave had been to put down a carpet surface over the whole area. We were able to move light chairs (rather than pews) anywhere at will, so that informally, with everyone in a crowded semicircle on the floor or on chairs, we could sum up the whole day and recall songs, readings, prayers and celebrate the art, drama and music: a joyful expression of our collaborative learning.

Another natural development in encouraging the whole congregation to pray, rather than just the clergy, was to become much more flexible about the timing of weekday eucharists, enabling young parents actually to be encouraged to find convenient times and be relaxed, so that their toddlers felt at home in church together with the leisured and retired. Certainly the struggle has to be made to find plenty of time for prayer, eucharist and silence, if a priest is to have right judgement, but it should never be at the permanent expense of his family, and never assuming that the lay people have no potential to grow with him into maturity. I was grateful that I never had to pray alone in church because there were always those willing to share the experience of keeping periods of silence, saying the office and celebrating the eucharist midweek, so making prayer a strong foundation for so many other strands of parish life.

A third consideration on the matter of laying the foundations of right judgement for the clergy is the permanent
commitment to study. For some this may be a planned course
of reading, for others a course in clinical theology or regular
attendance at pastoral conferences. Probably none of us
spends enough time reading novels or visiting the cinema.
The commitment of the Church of England to continual
Ministerial education is expressed in the growth of clerical
assessment and accountability, and the allocation of an
annual sum to be used by individuals, whatever the need is
perceived to be. This is certainly giving confidence to those
who run national courses, who recognize that there is a
market with spending power.

I needed to read methodically, by writing off several days
each month and disappearing to a library to be away from the
phone and the doorbell. I read widely within the growing
stream of literature that over the past decade has been
helping to fix the theological principles on which our
churches' lives can be built. This gave me the confidence to
continue, through many difficulties, to trust my judgement
in a confused maze of expectations and human inadequacies,
both within the community and within myself.

The role of the clergy wife is often discussed and has
recently been going through some changes. I know of priests
who, having moved from another career to ordination, have
to work through the confusion this causes both for themselves and their wives. One wife said to me recently, about
her curate husband who never seemed to have an evening at
home, "I do want him to do his new work properly but surely
he should be at home sometimes too. I just don't know what I
should expect". Her remarks contain a combination of
puzzlement, anger and guilt. With loyalty and excitement
she had supported and accompanied her husband as he took
the plunge from a conventional way of life to theological
college, where there had been lots of support for wives, and

so to the new parish and ordained ministry. Now, all of a sudden, she felt isolated, with small children at home, recognizing that the home of the assistant priest, unlike the vicarage, is not an automatic focus or crossroads for parish life.

Speaking for myself, I could not have survived in the stress situations of urban ministry without taking responsibility for the management of my diary. A constantly open dialogue, with many renegotiated settlements with my wife about time and sharing the care of our children, was both a necessity for the marriage and an invaluable personal growth point. I met Claire when I was an assistant priest and so, unlike many clergy today, there wasn't a time in our marriage when I was a layman. That coloured our expectation that my work would always have a very high priority, and family life would usually fit round it. I know I have found many occasions when there have been impossible decisions to take and the family usually seems to lose. For example, if I've been away for a few days on a retreat or training course, it would make sense to have an evening at home to relax, catch up on what everyone else has been doing, and to share new insights. But for any group of busy clergy and lay people to find a mutually convenient evening to meet to plan something to a deadline is difficult, and sometimes you have to be the one who agrees to fit in, which may rob you of that precious evening with the family. Or, while I'm away an emergency meeting has to be fixed by others with whom I am working, about an issue that directly concerns me or which needs my contribution. Well, that's fine if it has to be, but it cuts down the evening by half. But then, unfortunately, someone who relies on me as a spiritual director had already rung just before I went away, when it was too late for me to see her, to say that some dreadful tragedy had befallen the family, and I could see no other course but to agree to see her as soon as I got back. So our family loses again.

Making decisions about such cases is bound to be difficult, but it's essential to recognize what is happening and constantly try to plan in our diaries to have time for our wives and families and to allow room to take in unexpected emergencies and funerals and the time-consuming and vital pastoral work that goes with them, because in reality week by week inevitably they do crop up. The danger is always that we take for granted the love and support of our wives and families, without even realizing what demands we are making, or whether we have invested energy in loving support for *them*.

I can hear an older generation of clergy wife, having read this, commenting that this is what they knew from the outset, that it is the Lord's work and their free and loving offering. My wife's understanding of the situation was that she was not ordained and therefore, like any other baptized member of the congregation, she was engaged in the process of searching to know what her particular baptismal vocation was. Therefore she gently but clearly resisted receiving a pre-packaged role given by parishioners, other clergy wives, or the way I chose to exercise my role as parish priest. She was genuinely asking the question, "What does God want *me* to do?" One way of examining this at the time was to look at another member of the congregation of about her own age, with a small family, and consider her as a model. If Susan or Mary could be expected to offer their particular contribution, what reasonable contribution could Claire make to the community's life? A great deal of release from resentment can come from allowing yourself to examine your gifts and choose to do what you believe God might be asking you to do, rather than gritting your teeth and having things thrust upon you, even when it's clear you don't have the necessary talents. For example, it might well be expected by some church-goers that the vicar's wife ought to lead the sewing group or the Mothers' Union, whereas in fact her fulfilment and gifts might well point towards her being secretary to the mission group or head of department in a comprehensive school. Of course, I am speaking very personally here and I know that many families would choose to order their lives quite differently. The vital word here is "choose". Although the servant model is essential for Christian ministry, we have to decide how far we as individuals can be free to be at the service of others, rather than merely conforming to other people's expectations of us, and always noticing how far our actions are making inappropriate demands on our families.

To balance out what may seem an idealized portrait, it's important to stress that, like any other Christian, all clergy wives are likely, if they're honest, to struggle through many fluctuations in their understanding of and commitment to the faith that their husbands, in very bald terms, are paid to teach and inspire others to follow. It is not made easier by other members of the congregation unrealistically expecting clergy and their wives to have superhuman marriages that do not require the same looking after as anyone else's. It does, however, make sense of a sharp episcopal interrogation, reported some years ago, of an ordinand and his wife. They were startled by the bishop's question, addressed to the woman, "And do you love the Lord as much as he does?" Yet if she doesn't, it will be hard to cope with the tough spiritual and physical demands that will constantly be made.

My wife reminds me that, like the wives of all men who work from home, she often has to answer the phone and the doorbell in my absence, acting as messenger, receptionist, counsellor and secretary, at the same time as running a home and looking after the children. The most difficult part of that she found was accurately conveying both the content and level of feeling of messages for me, of receiving and absorbing people's anxieties and anger and, most difficult of all, judging which way I might be likely to respond to an enquiry or request. "Which model of ministering is he working on today, I wonder?": "Is he in a liberal, radical or post-liberal mood this week?" Again, many parishioners had to be made to realize that what was said in confidence to me would not automatically be known by my wife, though if they chose to trust her with confidences and problems, she could, like any friend, regard that as a privilege not to be abused.

At heart, like an increasing number of clergy wives, Claire tried to live the life of a committed laywoman, primarily a member of the congregation with three young children to bring up, but with some time for ministry within the parish. The hardest thing then is to be allowed to identify with the laity. When that was possible, it was valuable to me to have a lay view of things reflected back which could often be at odds with how the clergy thought particular projects were going. It is a common saying that clergy wives have a duty to be the most assiduous critic of sermons, the development of eccentric mannerisms and parsonical voices, and I'm sure that's true, provided our wives pick the right moment. But there are so many times when we return home raw from a meeting that has gone badly, excited about a decision that seems right, confused or bitter about a personal relationship that has gone wrong, when a loving wife can listen, console and encourage. So often we priests find it so difficult to reveal our vulnerability, so that the people among whom we minister may be misled into thinking that we are always confident and full of hope and never hurt, whatever happens or whatever may be said to us. Our wives know us too well. Hopefully, women in ordained ministry will be able more easily to show their congregations how much they are sometimes hurt by them: the average clergyman finds it hard to show his true feelings in a group. I think probably our new understanding of our relationship with all God's people in the Church will gradually help us to learn to share our vulnerability more publicly, but I for one want to register my grateful thanks for the strength that comes from a constantly growing and changing marriage, that has blessed and deepened my ability to respond to my vocation to be a priest.

# 11

# A Church OF – Not FOR – People

For the majority of people in this country our churches are irrelevant, peripheral and seemingly only concerned with their own trivial pursuits. Those who at one time might well have been church members have found their "church" experiences in many other places: watching television, involvement in community care schemes, in parent-teacher associations, in sports and social clubs, and ecological and environmental pressure groups. It is time for the Church to become more truly local and available to a wider section of people on their terms, to be open not only to the listeners to Radio 3 and 4, but also to 1 and 2.

It is one thing for Church Councils to discuss mission, but quite another to be prepared radically to change their accustomed ways to create a psychological space into which a wide variety of people may enter and feel at home. An important way forward will be for churches increasingly to be led by local ministry teams, containing members both ordained and lay. Our planning needs to be biased towards making local churches more attractive and more available to more sections of society, without delay. But although we need to move with resolve, we also have to respect the pace at which people can receive a new vision, and acknowledge the existence of people at different stages of Christian maturity, even within one local church. Many are the disasters created by clergy or groups of excited laity full of zeal, but with an unwillingness or inability to listen or to be fully integrated into the business of building their church with patience and vulnerability.

Many priests are easily threatened by laity asking probing questions about parish policy, sometimes wrongly interpreting it as a deep personal criticism. All of us who lead in these new directions, clergy and laity alike, will only succeed to the extent that together we listen, pray, study, reflect in silence and remain critical of our most cherished policies, aware that the future will make even further demands that we cannot yet conceive. Essentially, ordained ministers need to begin to see ourselves primarily as one member of a team, though with a particular and representative task within it. The small group gathered for the eucharist during the week, the committee saying the office or keeping silence over the Bible reading, these are the places where the Church can hope to move closer to the vast majority of people in order to share in their sufferings and learn together to follow Jesus and the Gospel. We all know there are many in the Church who want to hang on to the certainties and securities of former generations, and who have the greatest suspicion or even disdain of so-called collaborative church life. Such people, especially when they have the confidence of class or wealth, can make striving towards a church that is of the grass roots seem insignificant or ridiculous, suggesting that the "real world" in so far as it wants a church at all, needs to see a strong, socially confident, all-embracing and respectable national church like a well turned out cricket team, a bastion of society. We must not allow such ideas to slacken our resolve or crack our nerve in searching for a renewed church that is *of* people rather than (however efficiently) *for* people.

To all who are disquietened by those who are resistant to the movement to rediscover the view of the Church that contains the vision of God in the world, through the life of a community of disciples of Jesus, I would offer these words of reassurance from two South American witnesses, Virgil Elizando and Leonardo Boff:

> The situation of these new experiences is like that of a young child beginning to take its first steps. Yet the older folk, rather than showing excitement about its efforts to walk, seem to be making every effort to step upon the young child and crush it. But the efforts to destroy it will not succeed. Its new life is not given to it by any human power, but by the very God who is calling the People out of death into a new existence.

This reinforces my own view that the churches of this country could find great benefit from listening much more to the voices of the worldwide Church, recognizing the inevitable limits placed upon our understanding of Christianity by our scientific, Western cultural environment.

I have not experienced them at first hand, but it may be that some new styles of being chaplain (lay or ordained) in a prison, a hospital, an industrial mission team, will be places where a true companionship with the "poor" that is truly non-patronizing, could be worked out experimentally. I mentioned that in the parish for which I was responsible, we had a Franciscan Discovery Fortnight teaching us a new love for Christ and an urgency to be concerned for sharing in his work in our continuing parish mission. I noted that the visiting mission team contained members of such a great variety that most people in the parish were able to find someone who made the Gospel true for them without denying their own culture. This could be a valuable model for the Church as a whole. How much we need a wide variety of style, cultures and language to allow far more people the psychological space, as I call it, to be able to explore

Christian discipleship as members of our churches.

Through the scheme we set up after our Discovery Fortnight, to try to harness the spiritual energy, and which we called Sharing the Faith, we hoped to guide and support various action groups to prepare parents who arrive with babies to be "done" so that they might come to a fuller understanding of what commitment they are making at a baptism; to prepare people of all ages to receive Holy Communion with appropriate understanding; to prepare couples for marriage; to get involved with the existing tenants' groups and other social supports on a vast housing estate; to offer to the prison chaplain all the support we can to former prisoners and their families; and to do far more to make known to the public that the Church is alive and at work and open to all. We tried hard not to revert to being a church *for* people, but *of* people, so that more members of the congregation were led, even newcomers and seventy-year-olds plus, to perceive and take up their own contribution to the church's mission, all the time trying not to be patronizing, not to cut people off because they are not middle class. Even in a church that has roots quite deep into working-class culture, there is the tendency for those who had "made it" with a house of their own and a bit of confidence to put down others who are not so successful or responsible. Once I was moved to join in protest with others in the parish at the threatened removal of our only community worker. In response, one local councillor denied the scale of the problems on the huge council estate in the parish, saying, "There is no problem. I was brought up there. Look at me. I got out."

In the Church we need to be creating for the future, it should be regarded as part of the normal programme that it can only regard itself as truly "apostolic" if it is making a genuine attempt to communicate with and include in its life the majority, rather than the minority of people, to relate the

Gospel to experienced social and community needs and to be involved in the struggle for a more healthy society. I admit that the church community in which I was the parish priest did not find out how to do this with much confidence, but increasingly in many churches there are clues lying around about this, such as the prime importance of keeping a wide social base, the need to offer a variety of opportunities for everyone to be converted and continually reconverted in mind and style of life, and to move forwards working and praying as a community, not merely as a collection of individuals. Listening and observing, we can see that the basic needs of people are to belong somewhere, to have work, food and health, housing and education for their children. In parts of Leeds, as in so many other cities, many thousands are impoverished in several if not most of these essentials. Merely caring for people has been the Church's past habit. It has not been a policy that has enabled them to become part of the church community or of the People of God, the Church, until they have resolved their problems, yet pastoral care clearly has a place in the total spectrum of what the local church reveals about the Kingdom.

There have been times when as an individual church leader I have fought tooth and nail to encourage the Christian community to include those whom the Church of England normally lets go, and yet have failed. From infant baptism requests and funerals among non-church families over the years, there sometimes came unusual and positive signals about continuing church membership. There were those who helped vigorously to spring clean the church, to work with the young people and generally to be part of the worshipping church. I remember the struggles I had some- times to help older, "respectable" established members of the congregation to share in "*my* mission" to these families, by allowing for differences in what language is suitable for addressing children, what constitutes a suitable meal or the elements of a day out at the seaside, or what minutes of meetings are necessary, how accounts are kept and even what they should be written on. I recall a great deal of first aid with some who saw the possibilities of church membership and other members of the congregation who tried to offer help with their marriages, their neurotic in-laws, their mentally subnormal children, their leaky water pipes and their transport problems.

Who can say what part the Church, the clergy, let alone God, played in that chapter of their lives, when they experimented with church membership? It would be easy to be cynical, shrug our shoulders and say, "It was ever so", and all over our country there are council estates in parishes in which not a single person belongs to the parish church. But it is to precisely this kind of situation that we must *all*, clergy and laity together, apply ourselves again and again until we come up with some more acceptable answers.

As I said earlier, it was my experience that when people have made the great effort to make it to home-ownership, they want to forget their roots and are not generous or well disposed towards others less fortunate who "live down there on the council estate". The society we live in reinforces such prejudices. Young people with hopes of promotion at work are seriously advised to move, because with certain post codes it is impossible to be looked upon favourably. It becomes convenient to assume that all social evils originate and are confined to "over there", and that it is not safe to go there after dark. "Respectable" parents are not keen on their children mixing with "that lot"; youth leaders need special encouragement to tolerate and facilitate a broad social mix; there are conflicts surrounding how much of a person needs to be "converted" before they can have a place in a church community. For example, is soft porn suitable reading for a would-be Christian or not, or is it all right as long as the clergy don't know about it? Out of supposed kindness, recognizing how far most clergy are out of touch with ordinary life because of their class background or their particular sort of detached spirituality, laity try to protect us from the hard facts of life. A double game often allows the priest to see only the acceptable side of people's lives. To avoid being like the Royal visitor who is greeted everywhere by the smell of new paint, I found the need deliberately to cut through this protective layer wherever possible, by making it clear that I knew more than clergy are given credit for. Then it became a tight-rope balancing act, such as Jesus experienced between the accusation of being too ascetic, like John the Baptist, or too worldly for people's liking.

Clergy often seem to be quite unaware of the difficulties faced by families they encourage to come regularly to church. I can remember not spotting in time that some adults could not read; not realizing how difficult it is for some to keep appointments; not feeling what it is like to dress and feed several children, and, quite contrary to local tradition, to walk uphill against wind and rain for twenty-five minutes early on a Sunday morning, with little more motivation than because "the vicar said we must". Although I was in that parish for over eight years and truly sought friendship as well as to be a priest, I came to recognize that I should never be anything but an incomer and "one of them" (i.e., a paid professional), even though reckoned to be "not a bad sort". You need to have grown up in any community to know how conversations *really* work, to be trusted, to see how families *really* interrelate, or to know which unspoken signals and silences are more significant than mere words. You are at far more of a disadvantage when you minister in an area whose history and culture is foreign to you. This leads to lots of questions about the value and likely success of clergy who increasingly in the future may be called out to serve in their home parish in such a context. But when you stop to consider how the wide variety of men and women in a Franciscan team visiting a parish provides someone to relate to just about everyone, largely because the brothers and sisters do not adopt a veneer of false culture on top of what comes naturally, does it not seem an attractive task to raise up local teams of leaders of varied styles, lay and ordained, women and men, with the same all-embracing possibilities?

But of course this raises the prior question of whether our churches are really prepared to take a new look at their expectations of leadership, ordained and lay. The attempt to explore a new spirit of worship, ministry and style of being the Church that you discover in many parishes now, is being held back by some who equate with Christianity the culture, the ethos of the Church of England as encapsulated at some point in history (Tudor, Victorian or Edwardian) and fight to defend it. In local churches we could instead learn to be proud to show that the faith may be expressed in lots of cultures, but never without a contemporary experience of the risen Christ, and that there are not a few in the know and the rest merely the simple faithful, the people, the barbarians. We have a long way to go to discover that merely conforming to the received pronunciation and the tradition as told to us by someone, and told to them before that, does not do justice to the potential which can be released when we aim to be truly the Church of God: godly, missionary and universal.

# 12

# Companions with Society

Like any church leader in honest or despairing mood, I have
vivid memories of the long procession of people who have
given the Church a chance – even if not, in our view, a fair
one – but have then gone on their way with very little
rejoicing. In my mind's eye, I can see, for example, a whole
family who gave up confirmation classes because I did not
spot in time that some of them could not write; the various
West Indian families, often with serious social problems,
who felt no sense of welcome or of being understood, and
who now play badminton on a Sunday instead of attending
the eucharist; the young people who have been confirmed
and then abandoned us so quickly; not least, the all too
numerous former members of our Guides and Youth Clubs
who are nursing babies alone and too young, in high-rise
council flats; the more elderly who yearn for a formality in
liturgy and life that we no longer dispense; and those for
whom we seem unbending and utterly lacking in friendliness
and emotion. Once we really see how boring and dried up is
so much that is rejected as "church", we are bound to want a
renewed vision.

As we reflect on the great nineteenth-century expansion of
missionary societies, and recognize how they unconsciously
exported Western culture with the Gospel (they could hardly
have done anything else), and when we recall how both
during the Crusades and in more recent times, the commission to convert the nations has looked more like a licence for

war and domination and the annihilation of other people's way of life, we are more than likely to experience a crisis of confidence. Comparative religion and sheer pragmatism in mixed religious areas leads us to be optimistic and generous in our assessment of other religions. Among church members a great deal of former religious missionary zeal is being currently channeled into organizations such as the World Development Movement and Christian Aid. And it is good that we have come to recognize this wider view of mission. Hopefully we shall begin slowly to recognize, without being naïvely romantic, how much we have to receive from dynamic forms of Christians, say in Africa, with their resounding worship and commitment to the wholeness of humanity, or from the evangelical and humanitarian spirit of Liberation Theology in Latin America.

The breadth of all this vision is very right, but there is a new danger of the Church becoming self-righteous about being the only group with the spiritual resources to teach humankind how to live in friendship, and brotherhood and sisterhood. This came over very clearly in the recent highly critical review of the work of modern theologians by Cardinal Ratzinger, who twenty years ago was regarded as a prominent, forward-looking theologian. Ratzinger disappointed many conscientious church members who are looking for the renewal of the missionary task, by making it seem that the official church has all the answers, and that the so-called "world" beyond the Church has none. To a degree, we might consider that there are many parts of our national political life, economic relations, defence, and foreign aid policies, where those who govern have privatized or forgotten any sense of the notion of Christian companionship. Yet in the words of Eamon Duffy, it is too pessimistic and arrogant of the Church to write off the world as "inhabited entirely by self-interested materialists, terrorists, pornographers, or concentration camp commandants". The world is where you and I and our neighbours live, work and seek our salvation. It is the same world for which Christ died.

Further, we must acknowledge that in other religions and in the world in general there is much that is life-giving and healthy; things the Church never dreamed of and can lay no claim to have initiated. It is humbling to observe how much the Church gets busy with its own private affairs while great human causes are promoted by others.

At one time in our parish in Leeds we were intrigued by the church growth engendered by an American evangelical organization which was finding quite a lot of favour in Britain. The idea was very simple: trained teams visit individuals and families who are on the edge of church life, and through a methodical and directed series of conversations attempt to bring them to a point of commitment and into church membership, and then on to training to start them visiting other people. The scheme boasted the need to plan ahead to enlarge church buildings, because of the projected rate of conversions and growth of the congregation. Having looked at this carefully, we distanced ourselves from it, although we had tried to re-interpret the language of a different theology of salvation from that with which we were more familiar. We abandoned it after thoughtful examination, because it seemed to have a real tendency to threaten and dominate people, but also because of its powerful world-denying character. Anything that people had been concerned with before their conversion seemed to be totally discounted rather than built upon. And that sort of dualism is not worthy of the church that worships the God whose Messiah is Jesus.

We found a much more authentic balance between asceticism and enjoyment of the world during our Discovery Fortnight, when we rubbed shoulders with the Franciscans amongst whom lively and emotional worship leads to a profound love both of God and his created order. An

Anglican priest, who is a local probation officer, helped us to see that it would be impertinent and patronizing of us, full of new fervour, to begin setting up Christian structures to *look after* the "poor" of the council estate. Far better for us to listen and observe where the community police constable has been beaten up, where the tenants already have an association, where community workers are in conversation with glue- and alcohol-abusers, where there is a local community transport committee, a group for single-parent families, old people's lunch clubs, Samaritans, marriage guidance and the like, and offer to lend talent and support to what they are already achieving. We have a lot to learn about the way we live together as Christian brothers and sisters before we are in a position to take over the world. Against all the churches, it is worth remembering the rumour, for instance, that when Father Leonardo Boff went to Rome a few years ago, he was accompanied by a Brazilian cardinal. The Cardinal is reported to have been bearing a letter from the Brazilian bishops' conference, asking John Paul II to reconsider the question of priestly celibacy in the light of the pastoral need for more priests. It is reported that the Pope tore up the letter in front of the Cardinal. This points to more than the inevitable failing among individuals but to an assumption about power, the same kind of power and formality you see from the outside in so many of our Church of England structures. It is easy to be pious about the organized church's spiritual contribution to the nations, whilst forgetting competely that it is only the deft handling of investments by the Church Commissioners at Millbank, with all the ethical minefields inevitably involved, that makes it possible to finance clergy stipends, pensions and housing. The World and the Church cannot be too simplistically divided: creation and stewardship of wealth in order to be the Church and to do mission brings its own tangled web of decisions and priorities.

Jesus' vision of the Father's love, which requires that we create a community that in love welcomes all, shares with everyone, joyfully serves one another at table, is possible for the world, but it can only be offered at parish level or in the dealings of international commerce in a spirit of humility. The Church's most significant gift to the world lies in renouncing the claim to be called "teacher", as though having all the answers. We need to remember that we bear Christ's treasure in earthen vessels, and that the God in whom we trust was most clearly revealed when Jesus was abandoned by his friends and so became the true companion of all for whom society has no plans and who seem to be living in the place where "God is not".

Those of us whose lives are daily and intimately bound up with the Church need to recognize that anything we say about it must have the characteristics of being modest, provisional and revealing a vulnerability springing from the gap between vision and practice. Analogies of the Church are useful, but if a single one is pressed too far or used too exclusively, it can cramp our vision. As Bishop David Jenkins once put it memorably, "The road to hell is paved with the bones of false dichotomies". The popular New Testament images of the Church as the People of God and the Body of Christ are used very widely today and have been of great service. The first picture of the Church as God's People stresses the fundamental dignity of all its members because of their baptism. The image of the Body reminds us of the inherent difference between the gifts and callings of individuals for the service of the Church and of its mission. But if either of these is pressed too far, to the exclusion of many others, the result can be a too small or limited model of God's dealings with us. It is all too easy to reduce our vision of the Church to something we can control, but which as a result may be too over-simplified or too easily defined.

This is true of the "ark" model prevalent among Roman

Catholics since the Reformation. It has clear associations with Noah and the flood, and indicates that you are either "in" or "out" of the Church. Officially, Vatican 2 has excluded such a simplistic, black and white understanding of the Church, and this has been of benefit also to other denominations who cannot recognize the God of the New Testament in such exclusivism. But the danger constantly lurks of equating the Church with Jesus' vision of the Kingdom of God. There are still Christians who cling to the notion of the Church as a city besieged and of society beyond as a place of sin, where God is not.

A senior church leader, invited to reflect on his experience as a young priest in wartime Europe, said he preferred the Nazis to the Communists because at least they kept the churches open. We are learning gradually to see that what pleases God is not how a society treats its churches, but whether or not it is committed to eradicating injustice on behalf of *all* people. This is the difference between a Church- and a Kingdom-orientated Christian mentality.

It is true that because of its very nature Christianity does imply some measure of withdrawal from and renunciation of the world for the building up of the faithful. But equally we must resist the pressure of powerful lobbies in society to reduce the Christian faith to the level of a private opinion or a harmless hobby separated from the "real" world of science, economics and politics.

There is also the danger that a church which exists as a sub-culture all too easily enters the lists with a prophetic voice as though having a monopoly on truth or ethics. Despite the urgent demands from some voices within and outside the churches, that leaders should speak out, there are others who recognize the sheer difficulty of knowing enough about a situation to make an easy judgement.

Another analogy of the Church which should be receiving high consideration today is that of "outcrop". According to this way of seeing things, the Kingdom preached by Jesus is like rock strata, present though largely invisible beneath the earth's surface, supporting and upholding the world. Just occasionally the rock will break through the earth's surface in a range of crags, a mountain or even a volcano. Here is the Church, the place where God's ever present loving concern is recognized and responded to, and where his name is glorified. So the "outcrop" analogy can help us to see that all that has the power to build up and restore human life is of God, whether those involved can find the words to give that experience a Christian label or not. As Schillebeeckx writes:

> Religions, churches, are not themselves salvation but a "sacrament" of the salvation that God brings about in his created world through the mediation of men and women in very particular contexts in which they live . . . Churches are the places where salvation from God is made a theme or put into words, confessed explicitly, proclaimed prophetically and celebrated liturgically . . . religions, churches, are the *anamnesis* i.e., the living recollection among us, of this universal, "tacit" but effective will to salvation and the absolute saving presence of God in the history of our world.

> *Jesus in Our Western Culture*

The present urgency for the Church to comprehend more fully its nature and its ministry is so that with more confidence and sense of purpose, Christian communities can make their contribution to God's cause, the salvation of the entire human family. In this task the Church needs the confidence of discerning what is its own particular contribution and also what can be done in collaboration with others.

All the time we must beware of blowing up the bridges that exist between the Church and others in our society, who are certainly not against Christ even if they do not fight explicitly under his banner. We must affirm much of what Karl Rahner was expressing in his phrase "anonymous Christianity". The Church's mission cannot be portrayed these days as a clarion call to distinguish between clear-cut truth and falsehood. We need to recognize as well as we can the presence of Christ at work in many places in the world, so that we can respond to the call to join him "within" and "alongside".

For Christians to spend time on moving towards a more flexible and open model of Church that encourages a deeper involvement in, and understanding of, the world, will not be wasted. Nor will the end result necessarily be introspective, because it could help the churches to become more fitted for the vital task of proclaiming hope in the midst of great darkness, perhaps even of responding to the call of God in all humility to the service of holding the world together.

# 13

# Clergy Working Together

My experience and observation lead me to suggest that on the one hand there are few things more taxing or spiritually dangerous for a priest than being in sole charge of a parish (or group of them), while on the other, working as part of a clerical team is full of hazards. I have, apart from a short period, counted myself fortunate since my ordination to have worked continually within such a team, both in parish and cathedral contexts. My main concern here is to try to set down some thoughts about the working relationship between a parish priest and an assistant curate. In particular, we need to ask this question: If the laity of the parish have been encouraged to share in ministry and the whole ethos is one of collegiality rather than hierarchy, what difference does that make to the traditionally received relationship between vicar and curate? Women ordained deacon with no immediate prospect of ordination to the priesthood will, I hope, find something of value here. In every practical matter of parish ministry, except with regard to the eucharistic presidency, women will, I hope, increasingly be treated both publicly and privately as equal members of ministry teams. It does no credit to the Church of England, during the period (however long it turns out to last) that we do not ordain women as priests, that we do not leave any stone unturned to give them equal opportunities for personal development and the expectation of increased responsibility proportional to experience and gifts.

172

There are many factors that have contributed to a fairly sudden breakdown of the expectations of the vicar-curate relationship that was still just in evidence in 1970 when I was ordained. Then the social prestige and real power of the incumbent was still evident, as a figure to be reckoned with both inside and outside the congregation. Curates usually began their careers in their mid-twenties, mostly with an exclusively academic background. They were often unmarried at this stage, could expect to do two curacies over a period of about seven years, were on a low income and received only token expenses of office. There are plenty of stories which flesh out this sort of situation. Where a number of bachelor curates lived in one house, the senior curate might have *The Times* passed on by the vicar after lunch, and the other curates could expect to see it the next day. A curate might expect to be told what time to go to bed and even have a sharp phone call from "the boss" if his light was seen to be on after the appointed hour. A visiting list might be produced for the assistant, with detailed responses to each visit required on a given day. A curate could expect to have his vicar give him clear instructions, for the sake of the parish, about when and where he might meet and entertain his fiancée. I know of one parish where the celibate vicar virtually stopped speaking to his curate who got engaged, with the remark, "We've never been used to having married clergy in this parish". A vicar could expect to demand that a curate would appear in church by a given time before Sunday worship, and feel quite at liberty, if he should turn up late, to send him away in disgrace with a remark such as "You're no use to me at this time of day". I have deliberately given provocative examples of the "apprentice" model of a vicar having "his" curate. There was, of course (because that's how the church ran its affairs in general until recently), a lack of power sharing, but it needs to be said most energetically that within that formal relationship there was often great comradeship, enjoyment and mutual respect. In fact, a small minority of curates and training clergy still collude in a relationship of very tight authority, and some senior clergy reproduce the model offered to them by their own training priests. However, I believe that to operate in a heavily hierarchical manner or to try to sell experience, is to fail to see how much has changed in the wider Church's thinking, in the way society operates and in the relationship between them.

At the present time, curates are often older and married when they are ordained, sometimes with a previous career behind them, better paid, more assured of a reasonable house and of satisfactory reimbursement of expenses. There are far fewer curates than there used to be, which means that where at one time there might have been two or three with a good training priest, now there may be only one or none at all. Also a three-year curacy is a more common duration, leading straight into membership of a team ministry or licensing as a parish priest.

The principle of collegiality, of sharing ministry among all the baptized, the laity, bishops, priests and deacons, is our constant frame of reference for thinking out afresh how the life of the Church should be ordered today. Classically, this was defined at the Second Vatican Council in the 1960s in terms of the right relationship that should exist between the Bishop of Rome and the College of Bishops, but its significance has been widely reflected upon at all levels of church life, notably in Cardinal Suenens' *Co-responsibility in the Church*, and is very relevant wherever two or more priests are working together in ministry. In *A Pastoral Guide to Canon Law* (1977) James Coriden, stressing that the priestly ministry is essentially collegial, writes:

> The Church is a Communion, a solidarity of baptized believers, a brother- and sisterhood, a

unique fellowship in Christ. It is served by ministries which are characteristically collegial, co-
operative, co-responsible – rather than isolated,
personal or monarchic.

The achievement of genuine collaboration requires that all
take on the nature of a servant, as revealed in the ministry of
Jesus himself.

According to the spirit of collegiality, the leader of any
Christian leadership team, however composed, can only be
regarded as first among equals. As the Roman Catholic
Church has learnt in recent decades, the Pope should not
come over as an international manager of all the local
churches if that implies that he is personally running their
affairs. Primarily he is bishop of his own local church, and
secondarily a focus of unity and a final point of reference for
all other churches, when required at times of uncertainty or
division. Collegiality does not permit him to act entirely on
his own behalf, but only in deep communion with the hearts
and minds of all the other bishops and clergy within the
whole Church. In the doctrine of collegiality, I believe we
have a key for how all groups of bishops, clergy and laity
should live and work together.

However, pragmatism so often takes precedence over
theology in day-to-day Church of England affairs at all
levels. While many senior priests with curates in training
would agree in principle that the old master-servant or
master-apprentice style is unnatural and inappropriate in
today's world, there is still a fair amount of pain around in
these relationships caused by the lack of a genuine commitment to thinking through the issues involved and making
positive changes.

The principle of collegiality assumes that a group of
bishops or priests or lay people working together have equal
responsibility and commitment, even though from an

organizational or hierarchical position, one acts as a figure-head or leader and may expect to remain longer in one place. Personally, I hesitate to make much use of the term "hierarchy" today. I know that basically it only means that all human societies need to be ordered or structured in some way or other to make them effective, but in our time it has unavoidable overtones which contrast unfavourably with ideas of sharing and come over more as interference or domination. If we dare to take the collegial principle as a given for two or three priests working together in a parish or group of parishes, it will not matter whether one of the priests may be stipendiary and another not, or that one may be very experienced and another recently ordained, because they all belong to the order of priesthood. Michael Evans, in *The Clergy Review*, writes:

> No priest is an island, not even if he is in a parish on his own. No priest is a self-contained unit, but is bound together by ordination with his brother priests.

Over the centuries the Church of England has been at pains to stress how much the orders of ministry mean to her theologically, and yet in practical and legal terms can be very inconsistent, especially with regard to the vicar's prerogatives. So often priests and parishes live as though there were a great prison wall or electric fence round "their" parish or "their" hospital. As we work towards the mutual sharing of specialized ministries, such attitudes need to be broken down so that clergy can regard themselves as essentially members of a team and within it contribute their own particular service. Many Church of England dioceses, in the light of agreed ecumenical theology of ministry and the Tiller Report (1983), are exploring ways in which within deaneries teams of clergy can work together rather than in defensive isolation, but until there is an agreement among priests to work collegially, there will only be frustration and tension. In the Church of England we often now see collegiality working among bishops, as in the recent statement on doctrine in the light of controversies surrounding the appointment of David Jenkins as Bishop of Durham. Within the college a fair measure of diversity can be tolerated. In an episcopal team of one or two bishops, one will actually be in charge, although regardless of experience or whether one or more are suffragans, and only one can be the diocesan bishop; nevertheless they are all part of the house or college of bishops. That is the collegial principle which the Church of England accepts, though I know that suffragan bishops vary in how they are treated! And yet in a parish, assistant priests are often treated as if they are on probation, not very committed, not very responsible or not expected to be there very long. In fairness, it has to be said there are teams where collegiality between priests flourishes and the Team Rector very rarely has any need to exercise "primacy", though I am here particularly discussing the situation of a parish priest either with one or more priests in training or with a non-stipendiary priest.

In Halton we assumed that all regular church members were committed, whilst recognizing the natural variations and fluctuations in faith of both laity and clergy. We tried, as many priests are doing, to work as a clerical team, sharing responsibility, even though there were natural contrasts in our length of experience, insights and personalities. This is equally true of laity in a congregation and of any group of bishops working as a team. The collegial principle makes no distinction in commitment because of age or experience, though you would expect someone newly ordained to spend their early years under the guidance of a more experienced priest, just as you would be very irresponsible to give a very new member of the laity heavy responsibilities in ministry, although this does happen where parishes are hard pressed, and it can cause pain when it goes wrong. Anyone new to a situation naturally requires plenty of time and space just to reflect on it all and to adjust. The senior leader in a group has the responsibility of making the necessary reflection possible by encouraging a curate to have plenty of time off, to go on retreat, and to continue some appropriate course of study. Here also diocesan officers for Continual Ministerial Education play an important role in encouraging the newly ordained to see training and assessment as a life-long process, to help them to know what national resources are available, and to press dioceses to make provision for financial assistance in their budgets. It sends out very un-collegial signals when assistant priests are expected to provide more financial subsidy for their in-service training than their senior colleagues, especially as they are more likely to be bringing up very young families.

One of the most difficult areas in the relationship between vicar and curate arises from the fact that the curate has not only perhaps several years of secular experience behind him as a teacher, shirt salesman, professional musician or scientist, but has very recently undergone an intense course of theological study. Coping with all the new knowledge that the curate can bring to a parish is not always easy either for the vicar or the people. I found that the curates I had responsibility for could often preach very helpful sermons or bring to parish strategy ideas which were new to me. It requires great sensitivity on the part of an assistant to "teach" the parish priest and the congregation new things in such a way that they can be helpfully received and acted upon in full view of the parish. Otherwise you get insidious remarks from members of the congregation like "Who's running this parish, him or you?", to which the short answer is "Neither of us"; but perhaps that's being perverse.

The model of authority in the parish a curate first works in will have profound positive and negative repercussions in the future, and despite the criticism I accepted as carefully as possible from my own curates, I am comforted to observe many "Halton" influences in the parish where one of them is now the incumbent. But reflecting on the importance of the recently completed training of the assistant priest raises the important question of what model he has seen there. The ACCM occasional paper (22), *Education for the Church's Ministry*, stresses that the atmosphere in college, the balance between activity and relaxation, the pressure to overwork, all have profound influence on the future work of the clergy. In a similar way we ought to look to colleges and courses, through the co-operation of all the staff, to provide working models of how decisions can be made corporately and how clergy and laity can work in collaboration.

There are many who would accept that all the priests on a parish staff are part of the priestly order, commissioned by the bishop to share with him in the oversight of the local church, guaranteeing collegiality, but who shrink from concelebration at the altar on Sundays. It seems to me common sense that the clergy who share together in maintaining the community in its apostolic faith and task should express that liturgically. I know some clergy who say that if they're not actually the celebrant, by which they mean the president at everyone's celebration, they prefer to help in a background way or even to sit in the congregation. We have to be flexible, and maybe sometimes there's something to be said for this, stressing that basically all of us belong to the People of God, but normally those priests who minister together in a parish during the week can best express this by being at the altar together on a Sunday, and this includes deacons, although they of course cannot concelebrate. Provided the priests take care in the way in which they bear themselves in public worship not to make it seem that their presence or contribution is somehow more important than anyone else's, and the symbolism of concelebration is kept simple and unfussy, it is natural and only common sense that they should reveal their order's contribution to the Church's life in this way. The need for sensitivity and working from a model of servanthood is not to be revealed by pretending not to be part of the order of priesthood, but rather by showing, in an appropriate way, that you are. I do not find it appropriate, for example, when clergy and servers engage in private and semi-audible prayers during what is meant to be an act of public worship. To be a priest is not to be more important than anyone else, but to accept the call to fulfil a role which the Church has need of. I doubt whether it is possible for a priest to be seen to be truly *"out of role"* regardless of what clothes he wears and how informal he tries to be.

The essential principle I hold to is that in the ministry and worship of the parish we should work more consistently to reveal that we operate on the collegial principle, but I should now like briefly to explore how parish priests and dioceses often get it wrong.

As a priest with a curate in training, I did all I could to support the newly ordained man in his strange new tasks, as well as to share with him my conviction that although our task was unique, because of our common baptism into God's people it was no more intrinsically important than anyone else's. Psychologically this was difficult for a curate to receive wholeheartedly. If he had given up a previous career, taken a stipend instead of a salary, and disrupted the lives of his wife and children, surely it was for something of overriding significance! Yes and no. This was compounded to some extent also by the fact that the laity were already engaged in many different aspects of ministry, some of which might traditionally have been the preserve of a curate. But I believed my task was to teach by discussion and by working together with the newly ordained. Although he would no doubt hope one day to be the president of some other church community, I treated a curate for the time being both as a dedicated member of the local church and as one with the responsibility, from day one, to share in the oversight of our community. I know some would say that a curate is not around long enough for this to happen effectively, but with the demise of second curacies some are staying longer, and many committed laity, because of their work, move in and out of church communities quite frequently too.

As far as possible, I attempted to permit the curates to share in the feel and the responsibility of presidency. For example, in his early days, I gave one curate, who had significant musical talents, complete responsibility for the parish's music and worship planning. I knew there was limited risk in this for all concerned, because he had expertise (gained from his life before ordination) in leading others in the performance of music in worship. Therefore he already had, as do many of today's assistant priests if only this were recognized, vital experience in managing people. A great deal of the work of priestly presidency inevitably includes the gift or charism of management, which can often include the ability to face rather than to sidestep conflict within the community. I believe it worked very well, though there were odd times when things went wrong. Lay people in confusion, or with simple questions about arrangements for worship, might still turn to me as "the boss", expecting me to know in detail what was happening, and sometimes made me feel anxious when I realized that I didn't always know. But that's the pain of truly letting go and sharing responsibility. Sometimes I would forget too, and make a decision that was not mine to make. I can think of an occasion when, as far as I was concerned, although I had worked with a curate and a group of laity on planning a children's day festival, I thought I had made it clear that the curate was in charge and that I might not be there. But there was uncertainty at the beginning of the day when I went in to see how many children had turned up, because that made it very unclear who was actually in charge and responsible for getting things going. I am aware of parishes where vicars have specifically invited assistants to set up projects that they know they could not mount themselves, say in drama or evangelism training, and then suddenly, when it either went very well or mistakes were made, got cold feet and misused their powers by suddenly aborting the whole enterprise or sadly revealing the human sin of envy of another's gifts or popularity.

There are problems which arise through the natural lack of experience of an assistant priest in dealing with specifically priestly tasks or confidences. In one parish I know of, the assistant needed a great deal of persuasion to take holidays. Eventually the vicar got to the bottom of it: the assistant had become so attached to one of his specific jobs, namely taking Holy Communion to the sick in a local hospital, that he could hardly imagine how a lay person or even his senior colleague might have the willingness, time or aptitude to take his place. In my own experience, I have at times returned from a short absence from the parish to be told of new developments in the pastoral scene. On one occasion a member of the congregation had persuaded a colleague that he was experiencing a call to the priesthood, and the director of ordinands in the diocese had already been contacted. I was naturally annoyed about this because, as the senior priest, that contact should have been made after consultation with me on my return. Also I was surprised because, although I would be the first to agree that within the ordained ministry we need a complete cross-section of human styles, we also require people who are showing signs of following their way of discipleship with some integrity. In that particular case, I felt it was obvious that that aspect was far from clear.

On another occasion I returned from holiday to find my assistant had embarked upon a high-powered course of pastoral action with an individual. The parishioner, whom I thought I recognized as being highly manipulative, attention-seeking and in some deep way mentally unbalanced, had persuaded my colleague that he was dying in the short term. I was immediately concerned that my colleague was giving such a great deal of time to this man, to the detriment of his other tasks, and was wanting to keep me out of the situation. It seemed to me that I was being told: "Please keep out of this one: I know what I'm doing. Let me get on with what I've been ordained to do." I knew that as his senior colleague, with responsibility for his initial training, I should not prevent him from having his own areas of responsibility, but that this couldn't be one of them. I had observed and spoken with the man for some months before my colleague came on the scene, and I had a deep intuition that all was not as he would have it appear. So I knew I had to keep involved personally. My colleague was initially very upset by my attitude. He recognized that within our relationship I was definitely senior, but that collegiality can become a nonsense when the senior one, instead of working in partnership with his assistant, simply works through him on a line management model. He saw the need in pastoral care to have particular areas of responsibility himself, not as a power base but as a bit of a garden to be looked after, so when I muscled in on this "crisis" because of the anxieties my experience alerted in me, he did not at first understand my motives. However, because I gently but definitely insisted, we did share the visiting and the caring until eventually, through discussion with doctors and among ourselves, we were together able to recognize the complexities of the manipulative and mental illness that was rooted there, rather than a physical problem likely to result in the man's death in the short term.

Again, if you are trying to work towards a collegiate relationship between the clergy in a parish team, it is most unhelpful if the senior priest makes far-reaching policy decisions either alone or with a standing committee of wardens and treasurer. Either all the clergy should be included in such planning or else only the most sparing use of such standing committees should be made. In these days of so many Church Council committees and even local ministry teams, it can seem very unhelpful to have an inner core who are really in on everything and deprive others of significant decision taking and responsibility. On the other hand, if a sensitive or confidential parish matter has to be tackled as an emergency, a meeting of clergy and wardens is the obvious place to discuss it. On the old master-apprentice model, the curate might hardly have dared to complain about inconsistencies in his senior colleague, because the training priest might not show sufficient vulnerability or openness, and, after all, he was in charge while the other was regarded as a "helper" rather than being given the dignity of co-responsibility. On occasions like this in today's parish priest-assistant priest relationship, bridges certainly have to be mended from both sides, and problems of inaccurate communication recognized and talked through. Weekly staff meetings between all the priests in a team are not so much about deciding who does what and when, but about sharing in and growing deeper into this collegiate relationship. If time was skimped on this, I soon recognized that we ended up merely working in tandem, rather than as a corporate body. And, as Cardinal Suenens has pointed out, the future lies with the younger parish priest who can deliberately strike out with a challenging, theologically thought-out strategy, offering his assistant the true dignity of a team member.

The newer generation of priests must learn from the beginning how to live and work as a team. They must experience solidarity and be introduced into a sense of co-responsibility which they can put into practice for the rest of their lives . . . . Priestly co-responsibility will not happen just by itself; it will be the responsibility of coming generations to bring it to life through the whole church.

*Co-responsibility in the Church*,
London 1968, pp. 134-5

This cannot be taken as automatically accepted. Only recently a parish priest in his mid-forties was telling me how his curate's wife had rung him to complain about the way she and her husband were being treated. Assuming the old ways of senior priests' authority, he said he was surprised at her not realizing the bad impression she was making, and wondered why her husband (his curate) hadn't pulled out the plug of the phone. We cannot assume that collegiality among priests is automatically taken for granted, and it is much harder for the assistant to work from his end

I remember one of my assistants expressing anxiety that I was in danger of making Halton so different in style from what is normal in the Church of England that it was unfair on the congregation and on my successor. I think I tried to absorb that as a colleague open to criticism. The other assistant priest who served the parish with me, reflecting on his traditional background and college experience, his appreciation of the new theology of ministry, and his actual experience in the parish, reflected on the refusal of some senior priests to be vulnerable to really shared ministry with their juniors:

> When Arthur (whoever he may be) says, "When I was myself a curate under the famous but [he says conspiratorially] rather odd Canon Syringe, who was [he gets louder] nevertheless the finest parish priest it has ever been my privilege . . ." he says it in such a way as to make it quite clear that his long experience makes him senior and superior to us

185

curates. I do not want to disparage his seniority: I want to respect his experience. But I also want to be his colleague and brother – yet (why?) he draws the line. His security is nourished by my subservience. So be it. What dismays me is that this attitude of Arthur's to curates is also evident in his dealings with lay people, many of whom are responsible and experienced people themselves.

Mark Woodruff, "Letter from Leeds"
in *New Fire*, Spring 1986

In the middle of all these serious considerations, let me say there is great fun and companionship to be had between a vicar and his assistant, and their respective families: producing pantomimes together and even dancing at them in outrageous costumes to the hysteria of the congregation in the audience, glad to get the better of their clergy for once; taking time off to have a pub lunch together; on bank holidays climbing mountains and getting lost in the mists of the Lake District; on parish holidays being thrown in the sea or covered in trifle by friendly teenagers; and seeing the funny side of parish life or difficult parishioners at staff meetings.

I should now like to examine briefly the difficulties caused within the Church of England's parish structures when a vacancy occurs because of the removal of a senior colleague from a team, leaving a curate to "hold the fort". If the collegial model is right for a parish, there is certainly a permanent need for one priest to be the one who is the focus of unity. If we recall the parallel of the relationships between the Pope and the College of Bishops, without the specifically Petrine ministry being sensitively exercised, collegiality is endangered. No one would think of deliberately leaving the papacy or even a diocese vacant of an overseer for a long period of time. Yet we have parish interregnums that last months and even years. The long-established master-apprentice model of vicar-curate has been reflected in the official church's dealing with the churchwardens during a vacancy, and the days when curates were appointed almost privately by their training vicars and therefore resigned when a new vicar came, are not very far away. I know of one parish where, when the vicar left, the churchwardens, encouraged by the system, assumed all responsibility and left the curate so high and dry that he soon moved off to another parish.

Today the situation can be very complex. In many ways the bishops, archdeacons, laity of the parish and surrounding incumbents all assume that the curate is "looking after the place", and tell him what a good experience it will have been when he later reflects on it. Yet the official legal provisions of the Church of England place responsibility with the wardens. I heard of one curate recent.y who, during a vacancy, invited his archdeacon to come and take a service, and was told that that was not his business, the assumption being that the churchwardens would administer the parish with the curate acting as chaplain. In fact, a few years ago I simply took this for granted myself, much to the annoyance of my priest colleague. Having been invited by my diocese to take part in a month-long piece of in-service training out of the parish, I simply announced to the Church Council that Father Phillip would be taking services and be available for advice and so on, but that in my absence the wardens had the overall responsibility. That was the formally recognized pattern of things in the Church of England, but it did not feel right to anyone in practice.

If in all the time before a vacancy the assistant priest has been increasingly working in a collegiate relationship with the senior priest, as is more and more the case, the way the church handles vacancies will need to be adapted to prevent confusion and hurt. At diocesan level, when a senior bishop retires or moves, the suffragan – who has in some way (depending on the exact circumstances) been sharing in a collegiate relationship – goes on in as non-authoritarian a way as possible, exercising the oversight alone, recognizing that temporarily he has to govern the diocese. Increasingly with the rise of shared ministry, I hope we shall see areas of church work continuing along the lines on which they have been developing, despite the comings and goings of new bishops and clergy. There is, of course, a rightful place for senior leaders to challenge, adapt and refine the situations they come into, but there should be no mental signboard immediately going up: "under entirely new management". That being so, in parishes where collegiality and shared ministry are really becoming established, it is quite wrong for a brake to be placed on all developments until a new vicar is appointed. This only reinforces the whole idea that the parish priest is to be the fount and origin of all initiative. During a vacancy it would not be helpful for major new projects to be started up, but there is an important level at which there should be, as far as possible, business as usual.

In a parish like Halton, where conditions are favourable for the reasons we have already examined, it would be extremely unhelpful at the beginning of a vacancy – as though ministerial patterns were the same as they might have been years ago – suddenly to draw up stumps and put everything on ice. What has in fact happened there, as I imagine in countless other places, is that with the support of the Rural Dean and diocesan staff, the assistant priest continued to act as it were from within the "presidential team", despite the obvious lack of a senior partner, and in close conjunction with the churchwardens. Instead of artificially dividing the work into pastoral care and services (curate) and administration, financial and legal affairs (wardens), they have continued much as before, where both clergy and laity feel responsible for the well-being and development of the parish in every sense. However, they all look forward to order being truly restored as another senior priest joins them to continue working on the model that has been worked towards through the love and hard work of the whole community. So, whilst awaiting a new vicar the normal work of the parish goes on, after some initial feelings of insecurity – the local ministry team training, the lay pastoral scheme, the baptism visiting and the reconstruction of the Lady Chapel – according to plans agreed with the diocese before the vacancy began.

I remember one diocesan synod discussion about the setting up of local ministry teams, when a senior incumbent said that if he became the vicar of a parish where there was such a scheme established, he would demolish it within a fortnight because he didn't approve. My reaction was to say that despite all the pressures caused by the lack of available clergy today, churchwardens need to have the confidence to say, "Please respect where we are and what we have worked for. If you come to our parish as our vicar, by all means bring your own gifts and ideas but listen to us and share your thinking with us at every stage. We deserve, indeed demand, that you respect us." Recognizing that for one reason or another I didn't always get the vicar-curate relationship right, I feel very strongly that it is vital that we work hard, both in reviewing legal understandings and in the reality of parish life, to discover a collegial relationship. The insights about local ministry teams to which some dioceses have been coming offer a picture of a team of which the parish priest, his special place acknowledged, is a member – plus any other stipendiary or licensed ministers working in or from the parish, and a number of lay people. Excited as many are about such a vision, I would guess that most senior members of clergy teams are still operating, even if unconsciously most of the time, as incumbent *plus* assistant. So, instead of risking taking the opportunity of providing a model of collegiality to inspire similar relationships within the life of the whole of the congregation, we end up instead building division ever more strongly into the church.

# 14

# Local Ministry Teams

What I have written so far springs from the interaction between my own ministry in a large urban parish, and the current thinking of many churches throughout the world. Further, the developments in lay ministry were all possible given that the existing parish structures were operated with great flexibility and with a reduction in the level of formal behaviour. From actual experience, particularly of small rural communities, there is evidence that entirely new structures are demanded by the problems of the church in some places.

Here I should like to reiterate the seeming rightness of the theology of baptism that stresses everyone's equal responsibility for collaborative ministry and sharing in Christ's mission, even though some will have more demanding tasks than others. As we examine the struggles of the early Church (in a more authoritarian world than our own) we can see how by the third century they had painstakingly come to an understanding of the life of God in which there is no inferiority or subordination between Father, Son and Holy Spirit. The interior life of the Trinity, understood by the Church through worship, leads to a perception of the Church as a communion of brothers and sisters, where each generously offers himself in service to another and no one dominates in the world's understanding of that word.

From such a great weight of evidence, from the New Testament, early church history and liturgy, recently much the object of ecumenical study, a church can only regard itself as part of the catholic Church if it is eucharistically centred. "The first and most important duty of the priest or bishop is to assemble the people of God", wrote Michael Sharkey in a Roman Catholic weekly journal. This implies more than gathering people under one roof.

A parish priest can use many strategies to encourage the congregation to stop merely observing worship done remotely on their behalf, but instead to understand its form and regularly to help to plan and execute it. Such an ideal can only become a reality in a parish where the priest makes it his priority to evoke and direct many interacting ministries. We have already noted that, because of reductions in clerical staffing levels, especially in country districts, many parishes experience the Sunday morning enigma of a priest touring from one eucharist to another. Apart from strengthening the division between clergy and laity, the scandal is increased by the fact that often the local congregation will have taken responsibility for the ministry of the word in one form or another, so giving credence to the impression that the ordained minister has a personal power which requires him to be at the altar merely to consecrate the elements. With unseemly haste, and little sense of recollection or of belonging to the community, such a presider over the eucharistic celebration can become a caricature of a priest, what one African clerical leader has described as a "sacramental filling station". F.R. Barry once prophesied:

> If it ever comes about that a clergyman is a man who "takes services" on Sundays but does not touch the lives of the people otherwise, it would change the whole character of the Church of England . . . and that change would not be for the better.

Apart from calling into question our present dilemma of

many villages depending on one priest, Barry's comment does not support the use of retired clergy for Sunday duty, which is at present a vital factor in shoring up the disintegrating parochial structure. The overwhelming sense of inadequacy of such a visiting massing priest is described in the following account of an extreme experience by a priest of St Edmund's House, Cambridge, who during a visit to Peru was invited to say mass for a tiny village three hours' drive by Land-Rover from the nearest town. He wrote in the *Clergy Review*:

> Sister Therese, who was resident in the village, had prepared a group for their first communion, mostly teenagers, but all the families turned out and filled the little church, which they had built themselves. Sister Therese looked after the first part of the mass (including the homily) and I took over at the offertory. Sister Mary had aught me enough Spanish to be able to say Canon 2, but that was as far as I could go. This village and many like it would only have a mass a couple of times a year; it was a mass I shall never forget and I felt very privileged to preside at it. Yet it made me even more seriously convinced of the pastoral mistake of allowing such a situation to exist.

The Church's primitive practice, the classical liturgical prayers, and Vatican 2, all support the view that something vital to the local church's life is lost when a priest merely comes in to preside at the eucharist, because fundamentally he is not part of that community. Such celebrations are imperfect because only someone who is the acknowledged leader of the community can lead the worship completely. Our practice should affirm the vital connection between presiding at the eucharist and a commitment to that local church's mission and total experience of being a community.

But equally, no community, whether urban or rural, should be regularly deprived of the eucharist or have to rely on the visits of outside priests or retired clergy to maintain regular eucharistic celebrations. Some country clergy are convinced that there is no problem here, claiming that a close group of small villages may see themselves as one community, requiring just one priest. I believe that for such groupings the idea of a local ministry team, containing one or more priests, is much more faithful to the earlier tradition and more appropriate for the needs of our day. The expressions "Christian community" or "local church" or "parish" are vague terms and capable of a variety of meanings. In recent years we have learnt to recognize the existence of a variety of focuses of Christian living besides the traditional parish, for example through Industrial Mission, through hospital, university and prison chaplaincies, through schools and more recently in the house church movement and in the work of non-stipendiary ministers. Although perhaps for the majority of church members the parish continues to be the normal "local church" experience, we should be taking far too narrow a view if we failed to recognize the true value of alternative Christian communities.

The Latin American and European experience of basic Christian communities has much to teach us about this. Basic communities exist throughout the Catholic world as a response out of impatience with those in authority in Rome, and as prophetic signs for the new style of church that has not yet been born. Some are frustrated by the refusal of the Curia to allow the whole People of God to take their proper share in the processes of decision-taking, and by clergy who treat the laity as of secondary importance, fit only to obey instructions. Basic communities shy away from a church that avoids conflict, both within its own life and with governments and individuals who oppress and marginalize sections of the community.

Positively, basic Christian communities look for involvement in the issues of the society around them and apply their faith to global issues. They are remarkable for their evangelical atmosphere, conveying a sense of informality, happiness, openness and companionship. Although often to be found in situations of great economic and social hardship, they frequently lack the bitterness that is often associated with purely political protest groups. A deliberate closeness to Gospel principles evokes a sharing of prayer, of Bible study, of problems, solutions and practical help. Active involvement is a notable feature of basic communities, and everyone is encouraged to take full part and make the group their own. In political and economic matters, they are energetically committed to changing the structures of society whenever these exploit or limit human development. Clergy and laity share in these groups to differing degrees according to circumstances, but the clergy are learning that it is Jesus and his Gospel, not they themselves, that lie at the centre of a Christian community. Fundamentally, it is the whole Christian community that is the subject of mission, ministry and theological thinking. Just as priests are part of the church but are coming to know their place, theologians are made to realize that qualifications and publications are secondary to involvement in the every-day experiences of their society and the ability to interpret them from the point of view of the Gospel. Gustavo Gutierrez has made an essential point when he notes that there is a need for theology that is not done as work during the day, but as reflection at the end of the working day. I believe that in the West our parishes can learn from the spirit of these basic communities.

Theologically, whatever size or type of church community we are talking about, whether traditional parish or a gathering of workers, it can be defined in the tension between being a gathering and yet a sending out of those who believe in the Word of God. Basic communities have gone some way towards defining themselves by their deeply felt conviction that church administrators should not presume to judge them from the outside merely in terms of size and numbers. Throughout the pre-Nicene Church it was held, evidently on the basis of Jewish models, that a community at which at least twelve fathers of families were assembled had the right to a priest or a community leader. We should not naïvely attempt to apply the same rule today, but it strengthens the case of a small group of parishioners resisting the attempt of those outside to amalgamate them into a multiple parish to share a tenth of the time of a parish priest.

Prominent Roman Catholic theologians with pastoral experience have given us three vital points of departure, in accordance with Vatican 2 principles, when considering whether a community should have a priest and the eucharist:

1. The right of every local church to be capable of doing all that is necessary to realize its aim of becoming a community of disciples of Jesus and as such to be constantly growing. A built-up limitation is the requirement for the sake of catholicity that each local community is to be in union with and subject to the criticism of other local churches.

2. Quite simply the principle expressed at Vatican 2 that at the eucharist is the heart of a community of Christians, so it makes theological and pastoral nonsense if that community is regularly prevented from celebrating the Holy Communion.

3. The right of every local community to some form of specific leadership to clarify the given

196

dynamic power to the fundamental values of
the group or criticize the community.

Within the Roman Catholic Church in Europe the response
of local churches to the loss of their parish priest has often
been confident, articulate and positive. Just to examine one
instance chosen at random, let us see the experience of the
Italian community of Peretola and that of the Resurrection in
Florence, reported to a seminar held in Rome. Out of
impatience with those in authority in Rome and as a
prophetic sign of the new style of Church which they hoped
would one day be born, some of them decided that if the
system would not give them a priest they would work it out
for themselves. At first they invited several priests known to
them to celebrate when they could. But, dissatisfied with
this, they agreed that whoever led their eucharistic celebration really had to be one of their number in a complete sense.
They knew that throughout the Church's history the people
of God had delegated to a priest the task of celebrating the
eucharist as a sign of unity, but they felt that even in the
absence of an officially ordained priest, Christ would not
deny them the essential ability to celebrate the eucharist in
unity with God and with one another. Since then, they have
celebrated the eucharist among themselves, with the scrip-
tural readings, the prayers of the rite and so on. They
comment that they do not wish to set themselves up as a
model for others, but that far more important than adherence
to particular, historical conditions and rules about ordination, is the Christ-given ability of the community to
celebrate the Holy Communion. There is no doubt that
officials at the Vatican would condemn such action and deny
that it is a valid eucharistic celebration. The question is:
What is more important: church order about who may or
may not be ordained, or the possibility of every local
manifestation of the Church to do what churches need to do?

In the Netherlands, France, Spain, Germany and elsewhere, theologians, parish priests and local communities are looking earnestly for the day when canon lawyers and authorities in the Vatican will cease to place regulations and long held traditions above the community's profound commitment to the mission entrusted to every member of Jesus himself. They stress that as far as the New Testament is concerned, there exists the right of a community to have ministers to build it up and to celebrate the eucharist, and that it is the task of the Church in every age to create the structures necessary to make this possible.

Given the presence of such differences of approach in the Church, accompanied by significant numbers of unofficial actions and irregular situations, it is possible to make out a case that such a disorderly situation should be regarded as only a reflection of the normal way in which major changes have come about in times past. A situation in a local community which is at first condemned as "illegal" by the church's central and official leaders may in the course of time become dominant belief or practice in the Church as a whole, so that the original condemnation is evacuated of meaning. There are good reasons to see this as a fundamental strand of development in every age of the Church as new situations are responded to. There is always the danger in the institutional churches that a particular system, evolved in specific historical conditions, will become a fixed ideology because it is seen as venerable tradition. New and urgently needed alternative possibilities are more likely to emerge from the grass roots than from the hierarchy, because in every era it is there that theology, pastoral need and church law have to correspond to meet the fundamental needs of local communities in their Christian discipleship. Central administration is bound to lose its credibility when it tries to use force to maintain former traditions which are not central to Christian belief and which no longer carry intrinsic conviction.

In the Church of England there is a body of opinion, especially among evangelicals and within the Parish and People Movement, that lay members of communities should be permitted to celebrate the eucharist in the absence of a priest. The fundamental truth is, I believe, that faithful Christian communities will wither and die unless they find satisfactory ways of celebrating the eucharist: the sign which binds them to Christ and to one another in the Church. In the wide variety of ministerial patterns that we see emerging, it could be that lay presidency will turn out to be more than just an emergency cover in the absence of a priest, and become recognized as one legitimate way for communities to realize themselves fully. But it would certainly be against the church's view of ministry in the New Testament, in the early Church, in the Middle Ages and in modern times to suggest that just anyone should preside at the eucharist as a matter of chance or convenience. Personally, I believe that the question: "May a lay person do this or that and especially may he lead the celebration of Holy Communion?" is to misunderstand the nature of ministry. The practice of the Church down two thousand years indicates that a lay person who, because of his acknowledged leadership in the church, is called out by God, through the community, and who is specially commissioned by the bishop, as leader of the community, also to lead the celebration of Holy Communion, is in fact a priest and should be ordained. The experience and theological reflection of the wider Church suggests that there are places within the church in our own country which demand imaginative new departures from the traditional parish or local congregation being led by a priest or team of local clergy. It may well be right, as the Tiller Report within the Church of England has outlined, for small local congregations to work within a larger group, involving both stipendiary and non-stipendiary ministers together with lay leaders. Of course, in the Church of England there are many people whose spirituality is based primarily on non-eucharistic worship, and the infrequency of the celebration of the Holy Communion is regarded as a mark of its importance. Although the Oxford Movement and the Parish and People Movement have firmly established that the eucharist is central to the Church of England's worship, there are many parishes which for evangelistic reasons are offering as a main Sunday service once or twice a month, a short "family service", aimed especially at the less committed worshipper and young people. Sometimes I feel that we forget how complete a preaching of the Gospel the eucharist can be, if within its formal outline we use imagination and flexibility and thoroughly involve lay people of all ages. However, the point is that within the Church of England we should not argue for Local Ministry Teams including local non-stipendiary ministers, entirely along the Roman Catholic line of the need for more eucharists, although much of what we learn from Catholic principles and experience in the light of acute clergy shortages rings true. Local Ministry Teams do have the potential for building up the local church with more confident ministry, ministry that is not totally defined in terms of solo ministry of the clergy, ministry that is rooted in the local situation, but is informed by theological reflection, ministry that is an active symbol of the true character of the Church as the communion of those who are responding to God's call to repentance and mission.

There are growing numbers of dioceses within the Church of England moving basically on the same lines towards establishing local ministry teams which will contain stipendiary and non-stipendiary clergy, readers and a number of elected members of the congregation. There is no room here to go into all the details of how a parish might decide whether or not to appoint a local ministry team, how to elect its members, what training is appropriate for them and what their relationship would be with the Church Council. These and many other issues – such as the appropriateness of looking from the start for one or two members of a team to be called by the local church to ordination – are being worked out in collaboration with ACCM as schemes develop in various dioceses. However, the idea can be made clear by quoting two examples, one urban and one rural, from the Ripon report, *Local Ministry* (1983):

> In a city parish there are twelve people who, without formal training but with the prayer and goodwill of the church, visit the sick, the old and the bereaved. We do not think they should all be accredited local ministers. But their work needs support, co-ordination and advice, and it would be right to think of training and accrediting someone to enable the others to offer this ministry more effectively – a leading ministry.
>
> In a country parochial unit where numbers are much smaller, two people bear the brunt of similar work. One of them is particularly helpful in bereavement, the other competent in a more general way. To share in the team responsibility, to receive appropriate help through training and to be accredited could only equip these two better for their doing ministry.

In either case, the sensitivity of all the congregation to human needs of these kinds could only be heightened, rather than diminished, by this.

In my own former parish, which had known the sea-changes resulting from the successively different styles of ministry of in-coming clergy, we were glad to adopt the diocesan scheme for Local Ministry. Instead of an informal group of laity working with the clergy, the scheme provided for the careful election of a local ministry team, of which the clergy would be part. After a series of discussion groups organized to explain the idea, and with the help of the diocesan officer for Local Ministry, ten people were elected by the parochial church council from a longer list of parish nominations. The result was almost predictable, representing for the most part the leaders of many aspects of lay ministry already existing in the congregation: leading intercessions, reading, visiting, preparing couples for marriage and their children's baptism, preparation for confirmation and work among young people. The difference was that there was a structure approved of by the diocesan bishop, which hardly changed anything but added weight psychologically both to the lay leaders and the congregation's confidence in them. Added to this, the diocese has provided an outside tutor to supervise the team, including the vicar and curate, in a two-year general training course of experience-based theology. This course has especially in mind those who have little experience or expertise in formal education. At the end of the two years, the parish will be officially recognized as having a local ministry team, though there is no accreditation of the individuals within it. And a long-term lower key training programme will continue into the future. It was at this point, having laid the foundation for and supervised the election of the local ministry team, that I felt it right to leave the parish, after eight and a half years. As inescapably an itinerant rather than a permanent local priest, I knew that the time would come when I should have to leave. It felt right at that time to move to a job as Diocesan Missioner, where I could encourage many parishes to begin to engage in collaborative styles of mission and ministry. Within the system we have regarding clergy appointments, we must remain trusting and open that those with responsibilities for diocesan oversight will remain faithful and sensitive to what church communities like the people of Halton are more and more experiencing. Increasingly I hope that whole church communities will have a say in the choice of their ordained leaders and hence their future development. It is my belief that local ministry teams will contribute strongly to that process, although they should be very flexibly set up and operated, depending on the needs of the parish concerned.

I see the long-term solution to our present needs very largely in terms of calling and training groups of men and women who are already sharing in the oversight or presidency of a local church. Hopefully, suitable members of these teams would be asked by their local church to offer themselves for ordination as non-stipendiary, deacon or priest, to fulfil particular needs and roles in communities where their history and faith is known and respected. The Lichfield Working Party Report on Local Ministry offers an example of how this might work out in practice:

> Taking as our model the small village community with no resident vicar, we would suggest that the Christian community be asked to nominate a locally acceptable and willing person to be considered by the bishop for ordination. Although it might be possible to train and ordain such a person to a restricted ministry, we prefer the idea of a careful licence, which recognizes a valid ministry in the local situation but not outside it. Such persons should be clear from the start that there can be no guarantee of priestly ministry should their circumstances change, as, for example, by moving to a new area. In this way, a local need is satisfied and in a rural area of five or six parishes, one or two stipendiary priests could form a team with three or four non-stipendiary local priests.

Experience bears out that many stipendiary clergy and congregations are sceptical, or at least ambivalent, about locally ordained ministry. For example, unsuitable local ministers would be a menace and difficult to remove, though the same is already true of existing incumbents and leading laity. This must be seen as a warning to congregations to be extremely careful in the discernment, selection and training of local ministry teams. Such training would be most appropriate within a team, so that the individual learns from the start to regard ordained ministry as rooted in the local community and not as his or her personal possession or function, and training should always be as local as possible to preserve at all costs the cultural foundations of the individual.

A second objection is that it is a pity to "clericalize" lay ministries or to risk taking away initiative among the rest of the community. Most parishes already experience this in one way or another. Formal training and the formation of a team approach might help to increase awareness of the dangers and actually reduce in practice the loneliness and isolation of ministerial leaders. Compared with the tensions created by the present reduction in numbers of ordained ministers, the risks involved in local ministry are minor. Local ministry has the potential to provide more priests, more really committed church members and communities, and more trained ministry which will serve the new vision of the Church rather than merely provide the sacraments for a passive laity. Candidates need to be selected from across a wide cultural spectrum and be given freedom to develop new styles of pastoral and liturgical creativity which break down the clerical-laity divide.

It is true that among those who have been ordained to various types of non-stipendiary ministry there is a definite tendency, arising largely from insecurity, for a high proportion of them to want to transfer and to make this their profession. This situation calls for the Church to work out more confidently the vital role which the non-stipendiary and locally ordained can play in the future, and to support individuals in their particular situations. It may take patient education as well as the necessity created by lack of clergy to convince some local communities of the positive value of accepting ordained leaders who remain in their normal occupation. As Michael Ramsey said in *The Christian Priest Today:*

> The development of a priesthood which combines a ministry of word and sacrament with employment in a secular profession should not be regarded as a modern fad but as a recovering of something both apostolic and primitive.

Despite all the practical difficulties, the day seems likely to come when a local ministry tea n could be the normal experience of most parishes, and the solo stipendiary clergyman a rare enigma indeed. Though to support and guide local ministry teams and non-stipendiary ministers, there will need to be theologically able and humanly wise stipendiary priests who can help churches to avoid narrow parochialism by acting as a link between the local church and the diocese.

There is bound to be some incomprehension in the early years regarding local ministry teams, especially among those who only look to the church for occasional services. Expressions like, "What, our son baptized by the butcher?", encapsulate the need for wide education and efforts to increase the familiarity of the general public with these ideas, on the path to acceptance. Regular church members will take time to adjust, but may be quick to discover the advantages, given a well trained non-stipendiary minister or local ministry team whom they can support as they grow in confidence. At the moment it may seem as if the parish or collection of congregations is reduced in significance, only to be offered a local ministry team perhaps with one or two members ordained, but as they become more wide-spread so the traditional model of a highly educated professional autocrat with the culture and confidence of education and class will be shattered and blended with a much richer and more representative mix of community culture. Education and spiritual growth among the whole People of God may in time lead parishes to be glad of priests and other ministers who are not of a separate class in society, who are not *over against* them or on behalf of them but who lead from within. This will mean a growth in maturity sufficient to renounce having the safety of being able to hide behind someone who is transient and different and comfortingly responsible for everything.

There are many question marks around the precise details of the development of local ministry teams that eventually begin to raise up among themselves local non-stipendiary clergy. However, I believe that our present theological understanding, together with current experience in many parts of the Church and the vision of a Church that is rooted in the needs of society, all cry out for such developments. Every care, however, must be taken by dioceses and local clergy to ponder and consult widely before exposing lay people to schemes that contain a real danger of failure, or which do not meet a real experienced local need. At the same time, there must be plenty of room for local churches to experiment boldly and widely to find ways of being the Church that are inclusive of so many people in Britain today who feel that the Church's style and message is irrelevant to their situation.

# 15

# Reclaiming the Church

If some of what I have set down in this book is not relevant just to the development of one particular parish but has some universal truth about it, we need to promote an increase in the proportion of priests who are local, indigenous, and "*of the people*". Though there will still be a need for stipendiary clergy, they will need to be selected because of their potential for bringing to existence a Church which is moving towards the theology implied by the concepts we have been discussing earlier. As the Ripon Diocesan Report, *Local Ministry* (1983), suggests:

A different if related need for stronger ministry may be felt in the very many parishes where (we may thankfully recognize) there is a marked renewal of life and vigour, the awakening of a new kind of church-consciousness – new that is to the Church of England in the present age. Where this is happening we find some if not all of a complex of changes: worship tends to be eucharistic, participatory, confident and joyful before God, rich in fellowship which can transcend human barriers; ideally the body is not inward looking and relates positively to the world around; such a church is supportive of troubled lives, cares for young and old, expects responsible generosity in all its people . . . difficult to define, this awakening is easy to recognize. It can be encouraged but not made to happen.

In the development of any community life it is possible to place side by side two statements: the state of affairs that presently exists and the state of affairs that we would like to exist. If you agree to change the second statement, in order to restore equilibrium, you have to make every effort to adjust the first. For Anglicans and Roman Catholics, and indeed for other churches, there is at present a crisis demanding an urgent engagement in this process in parish life. The new vision is possible because of the thrust of ecumenical theology in all its forms, as well as the need for the church to be as well equipped as possible to grow and to serve human need.

While it is possible to observe in many churches a great deal of renewed vision there certainly is no room for complacency. I would suggest six particular avenues that we all must continue to explore much more deeply as part of the continuing process of stimulating the evolution of models of the Church more in direct line with New Testament Christianity and increasingly appropriate for our times:

1. We are a long way from coming near it, but I believe that the Church is moving towards a theology and practice, a style of being, which does not require local people to adapt their culture to that of a centralized church. They *are* the Church in that place and their local variety of talents and insights are for the Church's enrichment. As an integral strand of being the Church in this way a local group of Christians should be seen to be becoming more involved and committed to the well-being of the neighbourhood, as companions in pilgrimage with all who earnestly desire the wholeness of the world. This is what true holiness leads to. If we have established that the ministry of all God's people is

not "helping" the clergy, nor merely a response to the lack of priests today, but is directly rooted in baptismal commitment to sharing in Christ's own ministry, then we can expect a new confidence and joy in the Church. Baptismal ministry takes away from lay people the right to be objectively critical of their parishes and clergy with remarks such as, "If only we had a different priest, this parish could really go somewhere"; or "Why is it that no one in this parish will do anything?" If our congregations are to grow up and become communities, they will have to leave that luxury behind. Sharing in Christ's ministry is not volunteering for a job, which we may offer as a favour with strings attached, nor as something extra to our ordinary secular life, nor because we happen to like the present vicar, or to have importance in the community or authority over others. All ministry is for the sake of others, as a response to our discipleship of Christ Jesus, and for the direct support of places in the world where God's Kingdom is being worked for, the opposing of those places in the world where God's will is being frustrated, or for the development of the Church as an apostolic community.

2. Such a church will not scorn or protect itself from the least adequate, the ex-prisoners, the unemployed, the illiterate, but rather will be trying in whatever small way to explore with them appropriate solutions to common problems. We have a long way to travel on this road after so many years of giving up on huge sections of the population. All the time we must struggle to avoid becoming an exclusive ghetto or detached from the world, and instead learn to be eagerly open to listening and embracing all who will join us. God does not allow us to choose our Christian friends: they are given to us by him.

As a priest in East Leeds it was a help that I knew something about life on a council estate, having been brought up on one myself over a period of more than fifteen years and having attended one of the earliest Grammar Schools to go comprehensive, even though university education and ordination itself automatically changes your class and frame of reference. This is reinforced by having a clergy family living in easily the largest house and garden, owning a new car, and having complete legal security of employment. There is an expectation that the priest and his family expect to live an upper-middle-class life, whatever their surroundings. During the time I and my family lived in Halton we had ten actual or attempted break-ins to our home and adjacent church buildings, but I was able to meet the problems and challenges of life in that parish head on, without too much fear, because I had a real memory of living in close association with relatively powerless people before. This is, I believe, still too rare within the ranks of the Church of England's ordained leadership.

3. When I became a vicar of that parish, I was committed to the Vatican 2 insights into the baptismal responsibility of every Christian for mission and ministry, with a positive and patient but challenging expectation of all who claimed allegiance to Christ through that community. I believe we need to hold in tension imaginative worship created by using many talents, supported by nurture in the truths and experiences of a Christian community, along with attempts to help people to be faithful disciples of Christ within their home and neighbourhood circumstances, and their work or lack of it. We need more stipendiary clergy whose insights and experience enable them to contribute to this possibility by their visiting church people at work or even working alongside them for a time, without getting in the way or being patronizing. Further, clergy and trusted lay people must be offering spiritual guidance that goes beyond teaching prayer techniques, important as they are, to helping people make a

true connection between the practice of the faith and their daily obligations and frustrations.

The growth of local ministry teams with the potential to throw up local ordained clergy offers a vital way forward in providing church representatives who really are part of the local community and intend to stay so. Although I believe we shall also always need stipendiary clergy, of these we must have a greater percentage who are really able to communicate with working-class congregations and parishes. All clergy need help to let go of the mistaken view that they are called to exercise solo responsibility for the success or failure of local church work, either in total span or minute detail. The work is in Christ's own hands and he wishes to share it with all God's people.

4. Sharing ministry inevitably involves good but streamlined administration. Though bureaucracy can generally kill church life if it is not undergirded by the eucharist, prayer, Bible study and a sense of humour. But planning groups, time consuming as they are, are indispensable if they are used well, to allow people to take seriously their God-given task of working with him. If a community of Christians is to begin to share in corporate decision taking and action, say in lively worship that expresses their faith or in partnership with local voluntary projects, rigorous theological reflection on the task, together with joint planning from the outset, is essential and a good use of time. Together with this, the urgency of some situations requires a willingness to be spontaneous, to recognize what loving concern and ability already exist and, regardless of normal parish routines, to throw up action groups as needed.

5. But no model of administration, devoid of faith or prayer of various kinds, will be of any use for bringing nearer the Kingdom. The conversion of heart that produces the spirit of

joy and forgiveness in a community or breaks down prejudice needs to be constantly rekindled in the Church's life. I believe that time and energy will be well used when members of local churches are offered regular spiritual guidance or sacramental confession, appropriate to their needs. The Church is not an efficient business organization that puts people second to the system, and yet how often, because its leaders do not always have the necessary relationship with the people, nor sound judgement to discern who has and who has not the right gifts for a particular task, someone gets put in the wrong slot and then despairs or feels guilty or the work of a whole community of people gets stifled.

6. The renewed thinking and working out of the way we should all be the people of God is bound to leave on the agenda for some time the problem of re-defining the role of the parish priest. There are many conceptions of the Church, its laity and priesthood, which provide the raw material for a new theology of Christian vocation and ordained ministry within it, though the Church of England cannot claim at the moment to have such a theology. Some would wish to return to the earliest Christian sources, examining the nature of the Christian community in the Bible and writings of the Fathers, while others prefer to begin with God as Creator and his presence in the world today. I believe that we need to give attention to both these starting points, holding them in tension, but that the primary one is to be in touch with what the earliest Christians were believing, saying and doing. Without a strong Christian community, built up by an appropriate form of ordained priesthood, the faith will not be taught, celebrated or shared. The question is: what sort of ordained ministry does the Church in our day require? This is a question which will need to be considered for some time to come, but for the present, the principle I see emerging is for the local church's president to collaborate with the

bishop, and where possible a ministry team, to maintain the Christian community true to its apostolic vision and task. Can we raise up priests from our parishes who can fulfil this role with a light touch, as a final resource, as those who pray for the gift of sound judgement, rather than relying on cultural or educational superiority, or hanging on to power through their own personal insecurity, or by capitulating to everyone else's desire to have a scapegoat?

*

In practical terms a great deal of my vision for the Church is summed up in the idea of "giving permission". The renewed understanding of the Church in theory and reality can be released into action by clergy and responsible lay people who are told, "Yes, it's all right: you can take yourself seriously and joyfully in this or that role." Literally, "to permit" means to "let go". There are so many ways in which a new confidence in all church members can unfreeze God's people for prayer, study, communion together, mission and action on many fronts. Imagine a church on Sunday morning when there has been a heavy storm during the night which has found a loose tile on the roof. As they come into church, some of the congregation will carefully step round the puddle on the floor and go to a seat. Others will immediately bring a mop and bucket and clear it up. I am not criticizing those who do not mop up the water. It's just that they don't have the community's "permission" to do so. They don't feel responsible, and don't know where the mop is kept anyway. But it's not their fault: no one has given them permission. This is a parable relevant to the whole spectrum of tasks I have discussed in the book concerning the Church and the Kingdom.

Through our baptism, God has given all of us permission to take ourselves seriously as his beloved and forgiven sons and daughters. God calls us constantly to stand unprotected before him and to give ourselves in vulnerability to our fellow Christians and to the whole world. We need no priest to give us permission to live out the faith with passionate commitment. However, many of us find it hard to believe that God truly loves us, warts an' all, so we find it hard to take ourselves seriously in prayer and worship. Through our human shyness and reserve, not wishing to push ourselves forward, our lack of confidence and knowledge of what we believe about God, we need a great deal of help if we are to become more effectively the people of God. A notable way in which this is happening is through renewal programmes and parish weekends. Through such experiences, away from "normal" place or routine, we are given "permission" to be more relaxed, emotional, show more fervour, enjoy laughter, allow worship to be stirring, to reach the parts other worship has not reached, to be more varied and treat children with dignity and as people. On one such weekend, when in a new way intimacy was clearly being experienced in a parish's church life, one of the participants exclaimed, "But this is just like Scouts!" What she meant was that having for decades been involved in Cub Scout activities as an Akela, often on training weekends and at camps she had experienced an informality in human relationships and a sense of fun and intimacy in worship which she did not associate with the parish's life and liturgy. The Church so often talks about community and family, but we could often get more experience of the Holy Spirit working through people at a conference of politicians or those wishing to study the breeding habits of frogs.

Clergy and senior laity, instead of hanging on to their responsibilities, should be freeing others for ministry by giving them permission to use their insights and to take risks. This applies to their witnessing to the truth at work and in the family, to their willingness to take a full part in the Parish Communion and prepare carefully beforehand, to feeling free to reshape the interior of church buildings to use them more effectively for contemporary worship, to express their emotions by using not only traditional hymns but choosing from the wide range of modern songs, to being free to take whatever seems helpful from various churches without worrying about party or denominational labels. As one parish with which I was involved recently concluded after a Pentecost study weekend:

Dear People of God in this congregation,
    It has come to our notice that you have many talents, including
        the ability to praise with all kinds of music;
        the ability to worship through silence;
        the ability to share love through touch and
            words and action;
        the ability to expound your faith through dance
            and drama;
        the ability to encounter each other through
            intellectual exchange;
        the ability to actively listen;
        the ability to teach and heal;
        the ability to paint and to draw, to sew and knit
            and to sculpt in our presence.

We hereby authorize you, in loving co-operation
with your parish priest, to assist in the worship
and mission of your church, making full use of the
aforesaid talents.

Yours affectionately,
God the Father, the Son and the Holy Spirit

It is my prayer that together, the People of God in all the churches, young and old, male and female, ordained and lay, will catch a new vision, a daring hope and a willingness to let the Spirit blow where it wills. Together let us begin the process of reclaiming the Church as the focus of the joyful responsibility of all Christians in their working with God for the good of all creation and the salvation of humankind. For this we shall need confident and hopeful initiatives from all individuals and groups who hold authority in the Church; we shall require many and varied experiments in worship, styles of Christian community, and methods of sharing in ministry, releasing the Spirit so that in ours and future generations God's word may be clearly heard. Through pain, humility, prayer and thought, God can make of us the Church he needs. It may be against our better judgement; it may not be the Church we would rather be. We may be confident only that in faith we have an important role to play, not as the world's teacher but as servant, recalling that God revealed his passionate concerns and his true self in the vulnerability of the Christ who died a criminal's death, deserted by his friends, outside the city gates.

# Recommended Reading

G. Alberigo and G. Gutierrez (Eds), "Where does the Church Stand?" *Concilium* No. 146, T. & T. Clark, 1981

P. Ball, *Journey Into Faith*, SPCK, 1984

L. Boff, *Church: Charism and Power*, SCM Press, 1985

L. Doohan, *The Lay Centred Church*, Winston Press, 1984

A.T. and R.P.C. Hanson, *The Identity of the Church: A Guide to Recognizing the Contemporary Church*, SCM Press, 1987

K. Leech, *Soul Friend*, Sheldon Press, 1977

G.A. Lindbeck, *The Nature of Doctrine: Religion and Theology in a Post-Liberal Age*, SPCK, 1984

J.B. Metz, *The Emergent Church: The Future of Christianity in a Post-Bourgeois Society*, SCM Press, 1981

N. Mitchell, OSB, *Mission and Ministry: History and Theology in the Sacrament of Order*, Michael Glazier, 1982

L. Newbigin, *Foolishness to the Greeks: The Gospel and Western Culture*, SPCK, 1986

W. Saris, *Towards a Living Church: Family and Community Catechesis*, Collins, 1980

E. Schillebeeckx, *The Church with a Human Face*, SCM Press, 1985

   *Jesus in our Western Culture: Mysticism, Ethics and Politics*, SCM Press, 1987

E. Schillebeeckx and J.B. Metz (Eds), "The Right of the Community to a Priest" *Concilium* No. 133, T. & T. Clark, 1980

L.J. Suenens, *Co-responsibility in the Church*, Burns & Oates, 1968

W.H. Vanstone, *Love's Endeavour, Love's Expense: The Response of Being to the Love of God*, Darton, Longman & Todd, 1977

    *All are Called: Towards a Theology of the Laity*, Church Information Office, 1985

*Also available in Fount Paperbacks*

# I Believe
## *Trevor Huddleston*

A simple, prayerful series of reflections on the phrases of the Creed. This is a beautiful testament of the strong, quiet inner faith of a man best known for his active role in the Church – and in the world.

# The Heart of the Christian Faith
## *Donald Coggan*

The author ". . . presents the essential core of Christianity in a marvellously simple and readable form, quite uncluttered by any excess of theological technicality."

*The Yorkshire Post*

# Be Still and Know
## *Michael Ramsey*

The former Archbishop of Canterbury looks at prayer in the New Testament, at what the early mystics could teach us about it, and at some practical aspects of Christian praying.

# Pilgrim's Progress
## *John Bunyan*

"A masterpiece which generation after generation of ordinary men and women have taken to their hearts."

*Hugh Ross Williamson*

# Also available in Fount Paperbacks

BOOKS BY C. S. LEWIS

## *The Abolition of Man*

'It is the most perfectly reasoned defence of Natural Law
(Morality) I have ever seen, or believe to exist.'

*Walter Hooper*

## *Mere Christianity*

'He has a quite unique power for making theology an attractive,
exciting and fascinating quest.'

*Times Literary Supplement*

## *God in the Dock*

'This little book . . . consists of some brilliant pieces . . . This is just
the kind of book to place into the hands of an intellectual doubter
. . . It has been an unalloyed pleasure to read.'

*Marcus Beverley, Christian Herald*

## *The Great Divorce*

'Mr Lewis has a rare talent for expressing spiritual truth in fresh
and striking imagery and with uncanny acumen . . . it contains
many flashes of deep insight and exposures of popular fallacies.'

*Church Times*

*Also available in Fount Paperbacks*

# BOOKS BY C. H. DODD

## The Authority of the Bible

"In what sense, if in any, may the Bible still be regarded as authority, and how are we to interpret the authority of Christ? These are the questions to which Professor Dodd addresses himself . . ."

*Expository Times*

## The Founder of Christianity

"A first-rate and fascinating book . . . a theological event."
*Times Literary Supplement*

## The Meaning of Paul for Today

Professor Dodd particularly seeks to bring out the permanent significance of Paul's thought, in modern terms, and in relation to the general interests and problems which occupy the mind of the present generation.

## The Parables of the Kingdom

"This book is a most thought-provoking . . . contribution to a very difficult subject."

*Methodist Recorder*

# Fount Paperbacks

Fount is one of the leading paperback publishers of religious books and below are some of its recent titles.

☐ GETHSEMANE  Martin Israel  £2.50
☐ HIS HEALING TOUCH  Michael Buckley  £2.50
☐ YES TO LIFE  David Clarke  £2.95
☐ THE DIVORCED CATHOLIC  Edmund Flood  £1.95
☐ THE WORLD WALKS BY  Sue Masham  £2.95
☐ C. S. LEWIS: THE MAN AND HIS GOD
    Richard Harries  £1.75
☐ BEING FRIENDS  Peter Levin  £2.95
☐ DON'T BE AFRAID TO SAY YOU'RE LONELY
    Christopher Martin  £2.50
☐ BASIL HUME: A PORTRAIT  Tony Castle (ed.)  £3.50
☐ TERRY WAITE: MAN WITH A MISSION
    Trevor Barnes  £2.95
☐ PRAYING THROUGH PARADOX  Charles Elliott  £2.50
☐ TIMELESS AT HEART  C. S. Lewis  £2.50
☐ THE POLITICS OF PARADISE  Frank Field  £3.50
☐ THE WOUNDED CITY  Trevor Barnes  £2.50
☐ THE SACRAMENT OF THE WORD  Donald Coggan  £2.95
☐ IS THERE ANYONE THERE?  Richard MacKenna  £1.95

All Fount paperbacks are available through your bookshop or newsagent, or they can be ordered by post from Fount Paperbacks, Cash Sales Department, G.P.O. Box 29, Douglas, Isle of Man. Please send purchase price plus 22p per book, maximum postage £3. Customers outside the UK send purchase price, plus 22p per book. Cheque, postal order or money order. No currency.

NAME  (Block  letters)_____

ADDRESS _____

_____

_____

While every effort is made to keep prices low, it is sometimes necessary to increase them at short notice. Fount Paperbacks reserve the right to show new retail prices on covers which may differ from those previously advertised in the text or elsewhere.